Littleha

1800 to 1940

Peter Walton, Jill Belchamber & Nina Twinn
Littlehampton History Research Group

©2022 Peter Walton, Jill Belchamber and Nina Twinn

The right of Peter Walton, Jill Belchamber and Nina Twinn
to be identified as the authors has been asserted by them in
accordance with the Copyright, Designs and Patents Act 1988.
All rights reserved. No part of this book may be reprinted
or reproduced or utilised in any form or by any electronic,
mechanical or other means, now known or hereinafter
invented, including photocopying and recording,
or in any information storage or retrieval system, without
permission in writing from the authors.
(folm@gmx.com)

ISBN 978-1-7392141-0-4
Design & layout: books@plant-ark.com
Cover image:
Swing bridge and ferry, Littlehampton Museum Collection

*Dedicated to the memory of David Twinn
who was involved in the conception
of the project but sadly passed away
before work started.*

Acknowledgements

We have had help from numerous people in working on this book. We have had generous support with information, picture research and fact-checking from Julia Edge, curator of the Littlehampton Museum. We should also like to thank Lucy Ashby and Chris Ansell of the current museum staff, and former curator Charlotte Burford who was involved in the conception of the project. We are very grateful for the use of photographs from the Museum's collections.

We thank Trevor Greaves for permission to use photographs from his personal collection and the National Library of Scotland for permission to reproduce extracts of Ordnance Survey maps.

We approached a number of people to critically review an earlier version of the book: we thank Len Barrett, Malcolm Belchamber, Neil Rogers-Davis, Michael Dolphin, Alan Gammon and Claire Lucas for their generosity with their time and their very helpful comments and suggestions. We are also grateful to members of the Arun East U3A Local History and Archaeology Group for discussions around slide shows based on the research for the book. We are, of course, solely responsible for mistakes in the published text.

Contents

Illustrations

Littlehampton 1800 to 1940

Preface

This is a book about context. It came about in part from a discussion of the need to make contextual information available to people looking at exhibits in the Littlehampton Museum so that they could better appreciate the significance of what they might be looking at. We were struck in working on our earlier publication *Famous Faces of Littlehampton* that context would also have been helpful in reading local history studies.

We have therefore tried to put together a narrative which analyses the evolution of Littlehampton since 1800. We have aimed to make a coherent story to help people understand how things happened and how this related to the wider UK economic and social evolution. Our analysis is done by strands, with each strand following a chronological pattern. Since the strands are inter-connected, this means a degree of duplication – the swing bridge for example is an important piece of infrastructure, but it is also part of the life of the river and its tolls ultimately flowed into the Council's pool of resources.

We would like to remind you that historical analysis is an imprecise art. The authors have to rely on different sources which are usually incomplete so the result is part fact and part conjecture. We cannot know either to what extent contemporary resources were biased or indeed ill-informed. We can only offer up this text as our best shot at understanding what happened from the resources available to us. We are sure people will disagree about some aspects, and others will remain unprovable.

Peter Walton, Jill Belchamber and Nina Twinn

The Authors

Peter Walton
is a career academic, now retired from teaching. He is an Emeritus Professor at the Open University Business School and a member of the Association of Business Historians. He has written many books and papers, including *The Blackpool Tower – a history,* and *Piers, Paddle-steamers and Profits* as well as collaborating on *Famous Faces of Littlehampton.*

Jill Belchamber
has lived in Littlehampton most of her life and taken a keen interest in its history. She is a committee member of the Littlehampton Local History Society. She worked on the Heritage project to document the history of Littlehampton's principal streets, and has been a volunteer at Littlehampton Museum. She wrote a monograph *The History of Littlehampton United Church* and also collaborated in *Famous Faces of Littlehampton.*

Nina Twinn
Nina was born in South Yorkshire and met her husband David when they were students. They worked in North and West Africa and then moved around Europe living in Hamburg, Paris and Madrid. They came to Littlehampton with their three children in the 1980s to be near relatives. Nina has taught in most of the primary schools locally and took on the history project when David passed away in 2021. She is currently writing the history of when and how her Russian father and Danish mother met in occupied Denmark during the Second World War.

The Designer: Ita McCobb
runs a publishing and design consultancy producing books and podcasts on plants, nature and related topics. Her background includes global postage-stamp and packaging design followed by book and magazine editing and production.

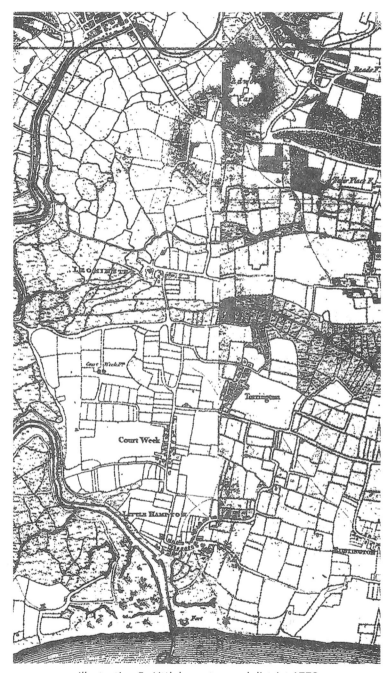

Illustration 5. Littlehampton and district 1778

Chapter 1

Introduction & Overview

We are setting out here to try to present a coherent story of the evolution of Littlehampton from 1800 to 1940. It became clear to us in working on an earlier local history project that, while there are several interesting studies that deal with particular aspects of Littlehampton history, there is no one book that tries to present an accessible and overarching history of the town.

There are several significant pieces of work that went in this direction in the past: notably Robert Elleray's history (1991) and Jack Thompson's series of short books called the Littlehampton Story, published between 1978 and 1983. Thompson included the text of an 1882 paper by Henry Lock, a Littlehampton schoolmaster, which gave a personal account of the town in the mid-nineteenth century. Both Thompson and Elleray also had access to Robinson and Heward's *Reminiscences of Littlehampton* published in 1933 with material by Challen which too drew on Lock's paper.

More recently these have been superseded by the Victoria History of the County of Sussex, Volume 5 part 2 *Littlehampton and District*, published by the University of London in 2009 (referred to hereafter as the 'Victoria County History'). This is an academic study covering about 2000 years of history. It has many insights about the land holding patterns of the area as well as its nineteenth and twentieth century development and has been very useful to us. It is, however, too large for the library shelf, expensive and not widely available. We hope our account will complement it by being more detailed in some areas and more widely accessible.

These studies are a solid foundation, especially the Victoria County History, but they lacked one great advantage available to us –documents archived on the internet. Material on the early part of the nineteenth century is particularly difficult to obtain, so past studies have been relatively light on this area. Our aim was to use on-line access to the British Newspaper Archive (amongst other sources) to obtain contemporary reports of what was happening in the town. We also had access to internet archives of trade directories (University of Leicester) ordnance survey maps (National Library of Scotland) and of course the British Library and the Open University library. Like our predecessors, we also were greatly helped by Littlehampton Museum as well as the West Sussex Record Office and West Sussex Library Service.

With encouragement from the then curator of Littlehampton Museum, we originally set out to research the history of Littlehampton from 1800 to 2020. However, we decided fairly early on that this would take a very long time, and that it would be more beneficial to aim for a more attainable target of 1800 to 1940, and then take on a second volume, or indeed pass the baton to others, for the 1940 to 2020 part. Part of our reasoning was also that this second period would likely involve different research resources – more local material is available, and people are still alive who can be interviewed etc – and would therefore present a different kind of task. Also 1940 was the date the Duchy of Norfolk sold its last holdings in Littlehampton, so marking the end of a particular relationship that shaped the town.

One hundred years of change

Littlehampton went through profound change during the 1800 to 1940 period, as did the whole of the United Kingdom. If we contrast the Littlehampton of 1830 with that of 1930, the differences are quite stark. In 1830 Littlehampton was largely controlled by the

Illustration 1. Town pump and Manor House

Duchy of Norfolk. It was a thriving seaport which was heavily involved in coastal trade, the main way of moving heavy goods or large quantities about the country at the time. It was also a gateway seaport for London, with goods transferred from ships to barges to navigate the Wey and Arun canal. It had an artillery battery at the mouth of the Arun on the east side, and was a centre for government patrols against smugglers. Smuggling of spirits and tobacco was rife at the time and many clashes with enforcement officers are reported in the newspapers.

Littlehampton was also a society hub, albeit not on the scale of Brighton or even Worthing. Eighteenth and nineteenth century society was convinced of the benefit to health of sea water, and it was customary for the wealthy to take houses by the sea for a lengthy period in the summer – often staying there till October. Littlehampton is usually referred to as a valued 'watering place' in the papers of the time. By this was meant that it was a good place to be by the water, or on the water or in the water for health reasons not, as it can now mean, a good place to drink - even if some people did think that drinking sea-water was also good for health.

From 1820 the Earl of Surrey (later the 13th Duke of Norfolk) established a household, called Surrey House, at the eastern end of Littlehampton (often known as Beach Town and centring on Norfolk Road). He and his wife and family spent a great deal of time there, as the court reports in the newspapers attest. They were visited often by the 12th Duke of Norfolk, and many other people were attracted to rent or buy the houses that had sprung up on South Terrace (which at that time ran from the Beach Hotel to Surrey House and was known as Beach Terrace). These included Lady Cecil Delafield, whose sister was married to the Chancellor of the Exchequer, another occasional visitor.

William IV was on the throne from 1830 to 1837 and held court occasionally at Brighton Pavilion, which gave an added social cachet. The *Morning Post* reports in 1835 for example that the Bishop of Worcester was staying in Littlehampton for the summer but went to Brighton to be presented to the king.

> ## Changing Names
>
> Over this period some of the place names have changed. In the newspapers we find:
> – Little Hampton, and then Little-Hampton and finally Littlehampton;
> – The first railway stopped at Leominster, not Lyminster;
> – The adjacent hamlet appears as Court Week, and only later as Wick;
> – Peregrine Phillips paid a visit in 1778 to Brighthelmstone, not Brighton

The Earl of Surrey was an active supporter of Littlehampton. He contributed substantially to having a carriageway built from South Terrace to the parish church (now Beach Road) and he sponsored horse races on the beach at Littlehampton, with his wife hosting a post-race dinner or ball. He was also a Member of Parliament for Sussex and involved with the Sussex Yeomanry. His father, the 12th Duke of Norfolk, was a yachtsman who both built and operated his yachts out of Littlehampton.

If we contrast this with the 1930s, Billy Butlin had just established a permanent fairground on land behind that previously occupied by the gun battery. An Odeon cinema had been built on the High Street (the town boasted two other cinemas) and Woolworths had just opened a branch in Surrey Street. Surrey House would shortly be demolished, and much of the Duchy's land sold. There is no longer any coastal trade; the canal to London is long gone, as well as the smugglers. The responsibility for roads, drainage and much else fell to an elected local authority, Littlehampton Urban District Council and the West Sussex County Council. There was a bridge across the Arun and the railway came almost into the town centre.

The 1931 census showed a population of Littlehampton of 10,435, compared to 1,625 in 1831. Littlehampton had become a favourite family seaside resort with probably at least 200 establishments offering accommodation, in addition to the hotels like the Beach, the Norfolk and the Dolphin which were already established in 1830.

Phases of development

The traditional analysis of the town starts from the perspective that what exists as a fully built-up area today can be seen as three different developments: the harbour, Manor Farm and Beach Town. A fourth centre, Wick, was added in 1901. Littlehampton was the point at which sea-going vessels could enter the River Arun and travel up to Arundel, going back to medieval times, when the castle was established. The main warehouses were in Arundel and the ships were protected from piracy or war by the necessity of navigating seven miles of river and by the implied threat of the castle.

Eventually a battery was built at the mouth of the river on the east bank in the eighteenth century, giving some protection and some ships preferred to offload at Littlehampton rather than face the tricky task of tacking up the river. Today, of course, there is no port at Arundel; over a long period, the harbour activity moved slowly to Littlehampton, which indeed came to be known as Arundel Port by some. There was shipbuilding along the river at Littlehampton and rope-making, as well as some fishing.

Manor Farm was the home farm of the Duchy of Norfolk (the Victoria County History says Hampton is Old English for home farm). It was back from the harbour area but not so far from it, and became the nucleus of a village, eventually connected to the harbour by Surrey Street and to the river crossing by Ferry Road. The Manor House, now the Littlehampton Museum and the Town Council offices, was built by the 12th Duke in 1827.

The third area was in effect a remote property development, accessible really only on horseback or by foot from Manor Farm. In 1790 the Earl of Berkeley built what Elleray (1991) describes as 'a secluded residence' at the eastern end of Littlehampton. In the following decades Norfolk Place and Norfolk Road would be established by the construction of houses, some at least built to rent out to wealthy people for their summer sojourns, and others offering accommodation. It became known as Beach Town, and represented the beginnings of Littlehampton as a resort.

Illustration 2. Surrey House and Norfolk Place c1860 (Greaves Collection)

By way of example, in 1856 there is an advertisement for sale by auction of three houses, 18 – 20 Beach Terrace, built as a lodging house and then used as a ladies' college. The houses had a 78-year lease from the Duchy of Norfolk remaining at that point. If we assume the original construction was based on a 99-year lease, that would imply they were built in 1835. These houses went through many changes, including later being a boys' school and again a hotel. The Duchess of Norfolk established a home for disabled soldiers during the First World War, and more recently the building has been a nursing home.

Berkeley House, according to Elleray, was later (1820) purchased by the Earl of Surrey, and renamed Surrey House. It is at least possible, even likely, that the Earl of Berkeley had bought a lease from the Duchy, rather than bought the land outright, and that this lease reverted to the Duchy. The newspapers refer to the house in the 1830s as the Earl of Surrey's 'maritime pavilion' or villa. In the evolution of Littlehampton we will refer to this period as the 'Sea' period: the time when everything was pretty well focussed on the sea and ships, either for commercial reasons or for health reasons.

The railway arrives

This focus slowly came to an end from the middle of the century, when the railway first came in 1846. We will refer to this second phase, from 1846 to 1914 as the 'railway destination' period. The railway dramatically changed the way people moved goods about the country and the way they travelled.

At the same time, the growth of the economy in the wake of the Industrial Revolution created many opportunities for people to generate wealth from manufacturing and to provide professional and other services. This in turn created new prosperity for some and much improved circumstances for others. A burgeoning middle class was created. Its members had money and wanted to enjoy a better quality of life, including stays by the sea.

The growing affluence also created a problem for London, that of smog. It is difficult to imagine now, but the widespread use of coal to heat houses led to air pollution on a massive scale. London could suffer from smog so dense that you could literally see only a few inches. This is the London of the Sherlock Holmes stories, also of Jack the Ripper. The air pollution was very bad for children and made life difficult for adults prone to chest complaints. It was 1956 before the Clean Air Act addressed the problem.

Illustration 3. Pier and river c1905 (Greaves Collection)

One of the means used to mitigate the damage of the smog was to send children to boarding school by the sea if possible, and to rent or buy a property near the sea for long stays in the summer. Famously Sir Hubert Parry came to Littlehampton in the 1880s for his wife's health and ended up building a house in Rustington. Members of the Garrett family, who were friends of the Parrys, rented a cottage in Rustington every summer. This was the period when houses started to be built between Manor Farm and the sea and Empress Maud Road was built between the river and the Beach Hotel as in effect the completion of South Terrace. A new and grander Beach Hotel was built.

Littlehampton in the railway period expanded significantly and became a watering place above all for the middle classes with its heyday between 1890 and 1914. It boasted few of the seaside amusements of places like Brighton or Blackpool but was popular as a family-friendly resort, and relatively easy of access from London by train. Alongside this, the spread of the train through France meant that the South of France was also much more easily accessible, taking a first tranche of the wealthiest away to the Mediterranean.

The town's port activity also flourished initially under the influence of the railway but eventually declined as ships came to be powered by steam: they were much larger and were inhibited by the shallow water and tide in the harbour. In the 1860s the railway company built a branch line back from Ford on the main Brighton to Chichester line and were able to bring freight trains along the east quay. This meant that freight arriving by sea could be transferred directly from the ship to the train without any intermediate transport. There were regular sailings to Honfleur and the Channel Islands, offering to transport goods directly to London via Littlehampton. There were also paddle steamers taking visitors on trips up and down the coast.

However, competition from the railway also caused the Wey and Arun canal to fall into disuse and it was closed as a commercial operation in the 1870s. Eventually commercial port traffic in Littlehampton declined after the 1880s, not least because the railway company decided to concentrate its efforts on the better harbour at Newhaven. Ship building and repair continued, but the nature of the ships was changing.

Local government develops

The 1848 Public Health Act introduced the requirement for parishes to form local Boards of Health. An inspection in 1852 recommended how Littlehampton should organise itself and a local board of health came into being in 1853. This was a major change in land management and urban development. For the first time an elected body was being given the right to raise taxes ('rates') on local landowners and the obligation to maintain public health by dealing with drainage and refuse disposal. While the first drains in Littlehampton had been instigated by the Duke of Norfolk in 1846, the subsequent ones would be put in place by the Board of Health and be paid for by local residents.

The 1872 Public Health Act reinforced the earlier legislation and made obligatory sanitary districts with boards to address issues like drinking water, street cleaning and sanitation. The Local Government Act 1888 introduced county councils, and was followed by the 1894 act which created urban and rural district councils. The development of town infrastructure started to be planned and managed through elected local representatives. Rosemary Hagedorn (2009) comments: 'The 15th Duke's death in 1917 heralded the end of the dukes as patrons, "rulers" and developers of the town'.

For Littlehampton as a resort, the arrival of Littlehampton Urban District Council (LUDC) meant that the facilities of the beach and green behind it were positively managed. It became a revenue-raiser for the LUDC but their management ensured its facilities grew and that it was a safe and pleasant place for holidaymakers.

Although Beach Town, at the eastward end of the beach, was the original location for holidaymakers, the focus moved westward until by 1914 the resort facilities were concentrated in the westward end of the beach where it meets the river, and the town had expanded to occupy all the land between the beach and the town centre.

By 1910 the demand for entertainment had reached the point where pop-up stages on the green were not enough. There was a rapid growth in pavilions as well as the arrival of cinema and even roller-skating. The Duke of Norfolk gave the town a new bandstand in Banjo Road and an area for tennis and similar sports.

As the population expanded, so did the church congregations, and this period saw a significant expansion in the number of faiths followed by different members of the population. There was also a major increase in the number of establishments offering holiday accommodation, and the range of accommodation offered. Boarding houses offered women a rare opportunity to own and run a business. The 1870 Education Act introduced compulsory education and fundamentally changed the provision of schools.

Creating a popular resort

World War I inevitably created a hiatus in the town's evolution. The economy was uncertain for some years after that as a result of the significant inflation generated by the war. This inter-war period, which we will style the 'Professional resort' period was a time when the town started to think of itself as primarily a seaside resort. The Council actively managed the holiday facilities and started to look to providing more resort infrastructure. There had been concert parties on the green before the war, using pop-up stages erected, as well as donkeys, Punch and Judy shows and bands. Just before the war there were various attempts to provide a shelter for live shows and cinemas started to open.

In this period the internal combustion engine started to compete more seriously with the railway. Now there were charabanc (bus) companies which would run tours to the seaside, as well as regular bus lines, such as the Southdown services, that offered an alternative means of travelling round the country and off on holiday. Lorries started to compete for freight. The old railway system, where goods were taken by train to a freight yard and then delivered locally by horse and cart, disappeared eventually

Illustration 4. Green and Foreshore c1933
(Littlehampton Museum Collection)

as lorries could pick up freight from its starting point and deliver it to its final destination with no trans-shipment.

The Littlehampton to be seen at the end of this period was not that much different from the core Littlehampton today. The main difference would be the massive infill of building to the east and north of the town. Of course, the Beach Hotel has disappeared, but the amusement park was built before the World War II. The Windmill cinema has developed from the pavilion on that site, even if the cinemas in town have gone.

The age of the motor car

The Littlehampton beach was out of bounds during World War II, which meant that there was little for visitors to do, but after the war, the business came back. Television was about to change people's lives but it did not change people's holiday destinations.

At major resorts like Blackpool, the arrival of television took away both some of the visitors' desire to see shows and the willingness of major performers to play twice nightly in person. That was not such an issue for Littlehampton for it had never depended on such attractions.

However, the traditional British seaside holiday was doomed nonetheless. The jet engine, developed during the war, was being adapted to passenger travel and eventually in the 1970s cheap travel to Spain with guaranteed sunshine started to become the norm. This was a great blow to the holiday accommodation business. Not only did visitors want sunshine but the new Spanish hotels accustomed them to having a bathroom of their own. Many boarding houses simply could not adapt to this big change in the market and went out of business. Many were eventually converted to self-catering accommodation.

Nonetheless, if one piece of technology changed the holiday world in a negative way, another was available to make a contribution: the private motor car. In our view, this period can be seen as the age of the motor car, where ownership of their own vehicle became feasible for many families. The traditional seaside holiday now meant piling into the car, rather than taking the train. Even when people started to forsake the traditional resorts for their main holiday, the motor car still meant that they could make daytrips or eventually weekend trips in addition to that holiday. So while some resort towns went into steep decline, Littlehampton managed to preserve some of its attraction with many weekend visitors.

Retirement

The other saving characteristic in Sussex was the fact that life expectancy was growing and people were interested both in retiring to a bungalow by the sea, and eventually being cared for in a nursing facility. Of course, these activities had existed for a long time, as for example, Rustington Convalescent Home demonstrates, being built in 1897. But new facilities were opened and some former boarding houses and hotels converted to this purpose. An example is 18-20 South Terrace, which was operated as Hillyers Hotel at the end of the nineteenth century, and had been a boys' school before that, but became a nursing home.

Some of the large houses were demolished and blocks of flats built in their place. This indeed was the fate of the Beach Hotel, that was demolished in the early 1990s and replaced by Beach Crescent flats.

The rest of the book

A fundamental problem when putting together a history book is that the writers have to make a choice between presenting the material by reference to the chronology, or by reference to other cross-cutting themes such as social life, business, World War I etc. Whichever way it is done, the reader is left with the problem of mapping across between different areas. We have chosen to provide an analysis by theme with chronology the secondary factor. We have done our best to link across chapters, but this approach to the analysis does involve some repetition.

How we are addressing the issue is to start out with this overview of the chronology, and then to present the material by reference to themes such as life on the river, the hospitality industry etc. We will start this analysis with a chapter on infrastructure which will to an extent populate the chronology with details of significant innovations that changed life in Littlehampton.

Conclusion

This chapter has aimed to serve as an introduction by providing a rapid overview of the town's evolution. We have tried to give the essence of its changing character by splitting time periods into:
1. Sea (1800-1850)
2. Railway destination (1850 to 1920)
3. Professional resort (1920 to 1940)

This split is necessarily arbitrary and makes gross simplifications. Many activities continued throughout the period, and where they did not, the switch from one emphasis to another would be gradual. Nonetheless, we like to think that this analysis helps to provide an overview, which can then be modified and lead to a more subtle understanding through the detailed chapters that follow. We are, of course, leaving consideration of subsequent periods (1950 to 2020) to a second volume.

Illustration 65. High Street
(Littlehampton Museum Collection)

Chapter 2

Infrastructure

Littlehampton in 1800

In 1832 Pigot's trade directory included an entry for Littlehampton which featured the following observation:

> *This place, which about twenty years since was nothing more than an insignificant fishing village, is now a sea-port of considerable importance, and, as a bathing place, annually advancing towards celebrity ... many fine buildings have been erected along the shore ... there are several inns, distinguished for the excellence of their accommodation ... the principal trade, besides that derived from visitors, is in coals and timber, which is carried on rather extensively.*

Over the period covered by this book Littlehampton changed radically from being the busy port and quiet watering place for the wealthy described by Pigot, to a town with a significant visitor business, based not only on stays in boarding houses and hotels but also daytrips from the surrounding area. The population grew from under one thousand to about ten thousand.

Many of the drivers for this change were changes in wider society such as the rapid expansion of the middle classes in Victorian Britain, significant technological advances such as the railways, and a transfer of stewardship from major landowners to democratically-elected local committees. Over this period the changes in the structure of society changed in effect the market for resort activities from a narrow privilege of the wealthy to something everyone in society aspired to.

The creation of democratically-elected local authorities provided organisations with a mandate to improve the local environment. The economic and technological changes affected the infrastructure and as a consequence impacted the way people lived, not least because transport and travel became very easy and relatively cheap. This chapter looks at what changes in Littlehampton's infrastructure took place and how they impacted its evolution.

Easy transport is such a feature of life in the twenty-first century that most people probably do not think of it as a significant constraint. However, in 1800 transport was anything but easy or cheap. If moving heavy goods, there was almost no choice but to use a coastal trader. There were hundreds of brigs, schooners and other boats, typically of less than 500 tons, which traded around the British Isles. The construction of the canals, which started in the eighteenth century, was the first significant change to that.

The roads were poorly maintained, since there was no formal structure to address that and little reason for landowners to spend money maintaining roads which would be used by others. Significant developments required a private members' bill in Parliament. There was some development of toll roads at this time, where people in a locality maintained the road and charged others for its use. Many 'turnpike trusts' were set up during the eighteenth century for this purpose. Nonetheless it was very difficult to take heavy goods by road, coaches had to struggle with poor conditions and the troublesome logistics of providing relays of fresh horses, which were the only source of mobile power. On the whole only wealthy people travelled for leisure purposes, and goods went by sea if they could.

Littlehampton benefitted from this to the extent that it was a seaport and centre for the coastal trade. The river Arun had long been used to convey goods to and from Arundel through

Littlehampton, and over time more and more shipping used Littlehampton and transhipped there. As a consequence, Littlehampton also became a centre for building the ships used in the coastal trade, and for shipowners such as Richard Isemongerand later Joseph Robinson who operated a fleet of such traders. The town was, however, restrained by the fact that oversight of its harbour, as a result of its historical development, was in the hands of harbour commissioners based on Arundel.

Smuggling was rife in the first half of the nineteenth century, mostly dealing in brandy and other spirits and tobacco. The newspapers are full of accounts of smugglers being caught either at sea or moving their cargo inland in this period. The government's efforts to defeat smuggling were initially directed by at least three different agencies but became concentrated in the Coastal Blockade Service under the Royal Navy, which eventually became the Coastguard Service later in the century when smuggling had abated significantly. Littlehampton had a Coastal Blockade Service office and harboured ships in its service.

Littlehampton also benefited from a seven-gun battery at the mouth of the river to protect it. Some documents suggest there was a battery there from the sixteenth century, but as John Goodwin (1985) points out, batteries were expensive to establish and the authorities would normally not provide one where the mouth of the river was not static. He suggests that a seven-gun battery of 18 pounders was built round about 1759 on the east bank of the mouth of the river and was intended to be able to fire on ships entering the river. However, the guns were small and the battery very lightly manned.

This battery should not be confused with the nineteenth century fort on the west bank which replaced it. The original battery stood at the mouth of the river, just behind today's coastguard station. The mound on which the cannon were mounted has been incorporated into the modern amusement park.

An idea of Littlehampton at the start of the period can be gained from the map at the beginning of the chapter. It is Littlehampton and district around 1780. The river Arun shows clearly and the road from Arundel to Littlehampton, taking in Leominster. It can be seen that Littlehampton itself at the time consists pretty well only of the High Street (then known as West Street), Arundel Road, East Street and Church Road (known as Berry Lane in the nineteenth century). Beach Road does not exist; indeed, Peregrine Phillips, whose diary described a visit to Littlehampton in 1778, tells of walking from the Beach Coffee House (eventually replaced by the Beach Hotel, in its turn replaced by Beach Crescent flats at the end of the twentieth century) into the centre of Littlehampton along a footpath.

Phillips comments that at this period people were already offering the use of bathing huts for visitors to bathe in the sea. He reports that one Monday morning during his visit there were four huts available and about 30 bathers. He notes that although the benefits to the health of sea air were well-known, people were now saying that immersion in the sea was even more beneficial. The landlord of the coffee house ('a good, honest, obliging fellow') also owned two of the bathing huts, made rope, went fishing and organised pleasure excursions in boats. Phillips comments that multiple occupation seemed to be the norm in Littlehampton, citing also the barber who was a lobster fisherman, harbour pilot and musician.

Phillips visited the artillery battery and was unimpressed with the casual nature of the arrangements. However, the Napoleonic wars (1803-1815) were to change that. It seems that the army built a new barracks at Littlehampton, and then proceeded to rotate military units through it and round the south east generally over the course of the war. Longstaff-Tyrell (2002) says that Littlehampton had a temporary barracks for 189 infantrymen in 1794, but barracks for 400 men were built in 1803.

Illustration 6. Dolphin Inn at corner of High Street and Surrey Street 1805
(Greaves Collection)

There are many military movements reported in the newspapers at the time. The *Hampshire Telegraph* of November 1807 reports that the South Hants Militia, quartered at Little Hampton received 200 men to 'make up their original number', which suggests that there were several hundred men in the Littlehampton barracks at that time.

The *Morning Chronicle* (Sept 1814) reported that the order had been given to dismantle the Littlehampton barracks. This was a little premature, as Napoleon escaped and re-entered France, before being beaten definitively at Waterloo, but the end of the war eventually put an end to a period where there must have been several hundred men quartered in Littlehampton and using its services. Nonetheless, officers from the barracks were thought to have been instrumental in the development of a Methodist congregation in 1816.

Goodwin (1985) is of the view that the battery was thought to be important in case the French forces decided to attempt to take Portsmouth from the land, by using Littlehampton as a beachhead. Nevertheless, he points out that the east bank battery was only defended on two sides and was susceptible to being easily taken over from behind by a raiding party.

Local government

The nineteenth century was to see a fundamental change in how infrastructure and other decisions were made at local level. At the start of the century the Duchy of Norfolk owned all the land in Littlehampton and nearly all infrastructure decisions were made (and paid for) by the Duchy. The only exception was the parish vestry. The Anglican parish structure was, aside from religious matters, also responsible for a number of issues including looking after the poor, keeping the peace and maintaining its roads. The 'vestry' was a regular meeting of parishioners, chaired by the vicar, which had an obligation to address these matters and the power to levy a 'rate' (local tax, still existing as council tax) on people occupying land in the parish.

Of course, parishioners were not all that keen to tax themselves highly, so elaborate plans to build quality roads for example were never seen. However, a significant duty was the payment of 'outdoor relief' to poor parishioners who could receive small payments from the vestry. This changed with the 1834 Poor Law Amendment Act, which encouraged 'indoor relief' in the form of the workhouse. It is a well-known element of local history that Littlehampton, in the form of St Mary's vestry, joined with other parishes to form the East Preston Union, a workhouse which was run jointly and enabled the parishes to meet their obligations.

St Mary's vestry was represented on the committee of the East Preston Union, and the Union's activities were debated in Littlehampton. However, the physical workhouse was in East Preston and we have decided not to address the history of the East Preston Union as a consequence. Its history is detailed in various publications, including the 2009 Victoria County History.

The civil powers of parish vestries declined throughout the century, disappearing eventually with the local government reforms of 1929.

Economic development

A major development for Littlehampton was the opening of the Wey and Arun canal in 1816. The Wey and Arun Canal Trust say that the canal had been built in order to provide an inland route between the naval base at Portsmouth and London. It connected to the river Arun which in turn connected to Portsmouth through the Chichester Canal. By the time it opened the Napoleonic wars were over and so coastal trade was safe, but the canal provided a new distribution route for goods coming into and out of Littlehampton. It was now possible for boats bringing, for example, coal to tranship to barges at Littlehampton for distribution further inland, and for barges to bring produce in from the countryside to be put into coastal boats and be traded round the country.

Population	
1801	584
1811	882
1821	1166
1831	1625
1841	2270
1851	2436

The canal caused a decline in the importance of Arundel and a significant increase in traffic at Littlehampton. The customs house was in Arundel, which became an inconvenience and Littlehampton shipowners and traders lobbied for there also to be a customs house in their harbour (*Sussex Advertiser* 1825). London wine merchants asked for the bonded wine store in Southampton to be closed and a new one to be opened in Littlehampton as being cheaper and easier for transfer to London (*Morning Herald*, April 1822).

The *Hampshire Chronicle* reports (March 1826) that very extensive works were carried out at the mouth of the River Arun to extend the piers[1] 900 feet into the sea. The object of the exercise was to increase the depth of the water in Littlehampton harbour. This was a continuing issue for the harbour users, as the depth of water at low tide inhibited larger ships from entering or leaving the harbour. It was in the end to lead to the decline of the harbour as sail gave way to steam and ships became larger.

In the nineteenth century there were oyster beds in the sea outside Worthing. Their presence attracted oyster-fishers from up and down the coast who often landed their catch in Littlehampton. The eventual decline and disappearance of the oyster beds would inevitably lead to the death of this aspect of harbour business.

If the harbour was controlled from Arundel, so also was the land around it. The Duchy of Norfolk owned all the land in Littlehampton and was as a consequence the arbiter of development of the land infrastructure. The control was evidenced in parliamentary debates on the 1832 Reform Act. This act brought about a major reform of the constituency boundaries in England. Its aim was to give parliamentary constituencies a more equal number of voters. At the time some notorious 'rotten' boroughs had very few voters and were thought to be easy to rig elections. Famously Old Sarum had only about six voters.

The 1832 bill attached Littlehampton to the parliamentary constituency of Arundel. This was queried in parliament where it was pointed out (*Morning Post* April 1832) that the proposed constituency jumped over parishes between Arundel and Littlehampton and attached only the latter to the Arundel constituency. Members suggested that as Littlehampton belonged to the Duke of Norfolk, this arrangement had been made to enable him to control the constituency the more

---

[1] The seaside pier as we know it today evolved in the second half of the nineteenth century. In 1826 what was built was probably a line of reinforcement more substantial than that which marks out the entry to the river today.

effectively. Defenders argued that Littlehampton, as the port of Arundel, was so bound up with the town as to be virtually part of it. The attachment did not survive.

The existence of a dominant landowner meant that much development could only be done with the support of that landowner, although this would change with the evolution of local authorities during the nineteenth century. A significant change in land infrastructure in Littlehampton took place in 1824 when a ferry was established across the Arun. Up to that point the lowest bridge across the Arun was at Arundel with the consequence that traffic moving East/West had necessarily to pass through Arundel. A particular problem was that Arundel sits on a hill, and therefore goods vehicles had to be drawn by enough horses to enable them to climb this hill.

A private members' bill was put before Parliament in 1821 to give permission to build a bridge at Littlehampton. This was strenuously opposed by the Arundel Harbour Commissioners and many other interests around Arundel, even if it was supported by the communities to the west of Littlehampton. Many petitions for and against were lodged in Parliament and eventually the proposal was thrown out in 1822.

In 1824 a ferry operated by a horse was proposed instead and a new private members' bill presented to Parliament. The *Morning Post* (Sept 1824) noted:

> *The very great accommodation the country around will derive from it is obvious. The road from Littlehampton to Bognor is through the town of Arundel, a circuitous route of fifteen miles, whereas over the ferry the distance will be only seven. There will be ... a direct line of road along the sea cost from Brighton to Shoreham, Worthing, Littlehampton and Bognor.*

There was little formal opposition to the bill and it received royal assent in 1824. Elleray (1991) says the ferry opened in 1825. The *Morning Post* later noted (September 1826):

HRH the Princess Augusta ... in improved health left Bognor on Thursday for Frogmore. During her stay in Sussex Her Royal Highness twice passed the River Arun in the ferry barge at Littlehampton and expressed herself highly pleased with the safety and quickness of the conveyance.

Illustration 7. The chain ferry (Greaves Collection)

The *Hampshire Telegraph* pointed out that when using the ferry 'not a hill is encountered in the whole distance along the coast'. The ferry would have brought through traffic into Littlehampton and supported the development of the town facilities, again probably to the detriment of Arundel.

The Earl of Surrey seems to have used frequently what the *Morning Post* described as his maritime villa, at the east end of Littlehampton, and forming the nucleus of Beach Town. He appears to have set up a permanent household there as well as using the Duchy's London house in St James's Square and other houses in different parts of the country. He was the Member of Parliament for West Sussex from 1832 to 1842, was a colonel in the Sussex yeomanry and took a keen interest in the local area. The presence of his household in Beach Town was very likely a major reason for the rapid development of that area in the first half of the nineteenth century.

In addition to attracting people to the area, the earl also encouraged development. He had paid for the construction of a new carriageway running from the Beach Hotel to the parish church - more or less today's Beach Road (*Brighton Gazette* August 1829). It was very much in the tradition of the time that such infrastructure improvements we paid for by the dominant landowner. The Earl of Surrey succeeded to the Dukedom in 1842 and moved to Arundel Castle.

The map below shows Littlehampton in 1852 (published in W H Challen 1933). Over the half-century, Beach Road has been built and connects the town with the beach and a bathing station, and South Terrace extends from the hotel along the front to Beach Town.

Illustration 8. Littlehampton in 1852

The railway arrives

The 1840s was a decade of great change in Littlehampton. The first railway line to Brighton opened in 1846, and was of course to change radically how people travelled and how freight was moved about the country. It would eventually lead to the harbour being used for regular services to France and the Channel Islands, and a significant increase in visitors. Pleasure steamers would eventually use the harbour; but the railway would also lead to the decline of the coastal freight trade and abandonment of the Wey and Arun Canal.

The Stockton and Darlington Railway, the first in the world, opened in September 1825. It was entirely conceived for freight: it was built to take coal from the pithead to the docks for distribution to the market by sea. George Stephenson was involved in building locomotives to haul the carriages. The most famous early locomotive, Stephenson's *Rocket*, won a competition to supply locomotives to the new Liverpool and Manchester Railway in 1829. Initially it was thought to be very daring for a person to travel on this dirty and dangerous equipment, but soon railways developed in an astonishingly fast way across the nation, handling both freight and passengers.

Development took place in a series of unrelated small ventures, a fact which would cause problems for the railways ever after and lead to many attempts to consolidate operations and eliminate redundant lines. Individual groups of investors would create a project for a single line (e.g. Brighton to Chichester) which would connect to other companies' lines at Brighton.

There was no national grid as such and inevitably duplications and awkward working compromises would arise. In Littlehampton this could be seen in the fact that the first line, opened in 1846, would link Brighton to Chichester, but would actually pass between Arundel and Littlehampton. These towns were initially served by a station at Lyminster (then spelled Leominster) where passengers and freight would be picked up by local carriers using horses and carts to be ferried north and south.

The construction of a railway line between London and Brighton was contested between different companies using different routes. Eventually, the London and Brighton Railway Company received parliamentary approval. Their scheme involved extending an existing line to Croydon down through Haywards Heath to Brighton - this remains the main route nearly 200 years later. The line opened in 1841 and soon had a coach operator offering a service once daily from Bognor to Brighton (using Littlehampton ferry) to meet the train to London (*Brighton Gazette* 7 October 1841).

A Parliamentary Bill was passed in July 1844 for the construction of a railway line from Brighton to Chichester. The first stage of building a railway is, of course, to obtain the rights to use the land. This often gave rise to expensive deals and indeed diversions to avoid unhelpful landowners. *The Standard* of 4 September 1844 reports on the annual general meeting of the railway company and quotes the chairman as saying:

> *Every interest set themselves in array against them, whether in the shape of landowners, turnpike trusts, proprietors of vested interests in the navigation, ferries or otherwise on the two rivers Adur and Arun.*

The chairman went on to report that the Duke of Norfolk had built a bridge across the Adur and been given the right by parliament to prevent anyone crossing the river for a mile above and below that point. The company paid him £42,000 to compensate him for the loss of tolls on the bridge. The sum reflected the original construction cost of the bridge. The Littlehampton Ferry Company also made a claim for loss of earnings, and parliament voted that if their receipts fell below 450 shillings in any of the five years from the opening of the railway, they should be compensated by the latter.

With the Brighton to Chichester line a significant problem was crossing the River Arun. The building of a bridge was strenuously opposed by Arundel harbour commissioners and a landowner, but they were overruled by parliament. That left the problem of building a bridge which would also allow shipping to travel up to Arundel. The railway company built, north of Littlehampton, what was described variously as a 'drawbridge' or a 'telescope bridge' – a section of bridge mounted on wheels which could be drawn back for shipping, similar in concept to the present-day retractable foot bridge connecting Rope Walk to the left bank in Littlehampton (actually the site of the 1826 ferry crossing and the 1908 swing bridge).

RAILWAY DRAWBRIDGE OVER THE ARUN, CALLED "THE TELESCOPE BRIDGE."—(CLOSED.)

Illustration 9. Drawing of retractable railway bridge at Ford

The *Southampton Herald* reported that a single line was completed from Brighton to Leominster in March 1846 and a service of six trains a day in each direction was started straight away. A second line of rails was in the process of being installed and the remainder of the line to Chichester would be opened in May. It added: 'Leominster is close to the main road between Arundel and Littlehampton, about two miles from each; and omnibuses run to and fro on the arrival and departure of trains.'

The *Brighton Gazette* of 11th March 1847 reported an accident between Angmering station and Littlehampton. The end carriage (a baggage car) of a Chichester train had broken its axle and dug into the track. No-one was injured, but the track – there was only a single track at that time – was made unusable. The paper reports that there was a Brighton train from Chichester waiting in Littlehampton station to take passengers east along the single track. It says the railway company told these passengers to walk to Angmering, where they could pick up a train to Brighton. The replacement bus service had not yet been invented.

The railway created an immediate demand for recreation, as this article in the *Brighton Gazette* shows:

THE FOLLIES OF A DAY

The utility of the railways has been averred by those who advocate recreation for persons the live-long week immersed in the toils of life. The opening of the Brighton and Chichester Railway, there is reason to believe, has greatly improved the pleasures as well as the business of the inhabitants in the vicinity of the line: and in all cases of pleasure-taking attended with propriety the argument of utility holds good. The following instance, however, of an excursion furnishes an exception. A respectable Brighton tradesman, with his wife, procuring the requisite of a day-ticket, set out by train on Saturday, on a visit to the interesting village of Littlehampton. Having comfortably settled themselves in a carriage comporting with their dignity, they were fortunate and happy enough to find in due course of ingenuous conversation, stimulated by the prospective joys of the trip, that two merry gentlemen in the same carriage were also bent on a day's recreation.

[They visited Littlehampton together, not forgetting to eat and drink, and then took the train back again.]

(At Worthing station) the gentlemen, on the stopping of the train, thought proper for the sake of variety to alight and soberly witness the exchange of passengers, leaving their lady companion in charge of their places. Essaying again

to join her, the station-clerk made the astute discovery that the (men) were staggering drunk. They were therefore politely restrained from completing their homeward journey, and obliged at a safe distance to waft adieus to their fair friend in the train, who, astonished, was swiftly removed from the view of her late co-mates. (August 1846)

Another major use of the train was also seen early on. A newspaper article noted that the train from Brighton to London took only an hour and fifteen minutes, making Brighton almost a suburb of London in commuting terms. The article went on to note that the line along the coast made travelling from other towns such as Worthing not an unthinkable journey to work either (*Brighton Gazette* 25 July 1850). In 1850 the railway company set up a wharf in the Arun at Ford, where goods could be transferred between ships and the train.

Public health

At that time the town was very basic in its waste arrangements. Henry Lock (reproduced in Thompson 1983) noted that at this time there was a pond in the town centre (in the area between the present-day Manor House and the shops opposite) into which all its waste was thrown. The pond drained off to the river and eventually the sea. It was protected from the tide by a sluice. Lock reports that village boys would occasionally open the sluice when the tide was coming in, causing the pond to flood and push sewage into the surrounding houses. However, in 1846/47 (*Brighton Gazette*) the 13th Duke of Norfolk had sewers built to improve the drainage in the main street. The 1801 population for Littlehampton is given as 584, but by 1841 this had grown to 2270, with a negative impact on the old arrangements.

1847 also saw the establishment of a gas factory in Littlehampton (*Brighton Gazette* 30 September 1847) which would have enabled a significant change in the quality of life. Gas enabled people (at least the better-off) to light their houses much more efficiently.

Later this would extend to using gas for heating which offered an escape from the work of bringing in coal and taking away ashes. Gas cookers would also arrive eventually and were considerably easier to control than coal ranges.

Gas in the nineteenth and early twentieth centuries was manufactured by extracting it from coal. This so-called 'town gas' therefore required a gasworks to produce it and gasometers to store it. One gasometer, albeit from the 1960s, remains at the time of writing in the railway yards behind the station. The gasometer is circular and consists of close-fitting bands under a heavy top, which lifts as gas is pumped in and preserves pressure. The gasometer feeds gas to the consumer circuit. Today we use 'natural gas' extracted from the earth and pumped around the country in underground pipelines. Town gas was explosive and dangerous, but also toxic, leading to death when inhaled in quantity. It was replaced by natural gas in the UK in the late 1960s.

The 1848 Public Health Act required that parishes set up an elected Board of Health to address issues such as drainage and removal of rubbish from towns and villages. Littlehampton's board was set up in 1853, under the initial chairmanship of Rev John Atkyns, with Stephen Olliver and J E Butt amongst the members.

In the next four years that board would extend the drainage scheme along the road to Worthing (presumably East Street and its continuance) and in Beach Town, taking the waste water to the river. The local board of health would thereafter be the focus of civic decision-making in the development of the town. It was also responsible for maintaining those roads which it 'adopted', giving rise to numerous negotiations with landowners and leaseholders about which roads it would look after.

It seems, however, that having set up a basic system of drainage the 'Local Board,' as it was generally known, failed subsequently to maintain the system or indeed extend it to cope with the increasing number of houses being built. The *West Sussex*

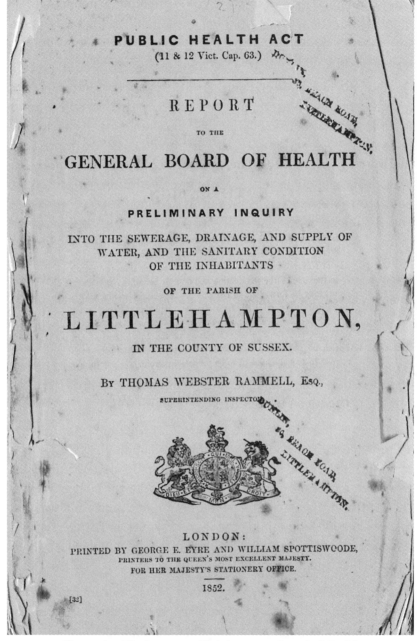

Illustration 10. Report on Littlehampton Board of Health
(Littlehamapton Museum Collection)

Gazette wrote in May 1870 of the many improvements to Littlehampton, including the construction of the promenade but also at least 100 new houses in the last year. Robert Bushby was a prominent builder in the town in the 1860s. Amongst other things he provided the foundations for the new spire at Chichester cathedral. He also built new houses and had installed some drainage.

However, he started complaining that the Local Board did not maintain the sewers, they were not watertight and in effect created cess pits near the houses. The Local Board did not address his concerns so he complained to the Home Office, which was the remedy provided in the Act. This incensed the Board and when the Home Office sent an inspector down in January 1871, they refused to meet the inspector or communicate with him in any way.

There followed a reprimand from the Home Office and the inspector came down again in April. He held a six-hour meeting at which all views were put forward. He was astonished to discover that the Board did not have any kind of map to show where the drains were, and wondered how they could be maintained without any kind of system. The Inspector also said he had to review the whole system of drainage, even though Mr Bushby's complaint referred specifically to Norfolk Road and Arundel Road. He said those cases could not be seen without reference to the surrounding system of which they were part. The Board disagreed.

The inspector eventually produced a report which was sent by the Home Office to the Board in July. This said that 'the system of main sewage is generally defective and deficient, the outflows are not low enough and are illegal in discharging into the River Arun'. It noted that the Duchy of Norfolk had offered to meet half the cost of improvements well before the inspection, but this had been turned down.

The Board was incandescent, replying that the inspector had exceeded his mandate by doing more than looking at the two roads, which had been referred to him. It said it would not consider the report until the Home Office had clarified the legal point. They also noted that Arundel discharged its sewage into the Arun, and large industrial towns were well known to discharge into rivers. Littlehampton's discharge was, furthermore, at the mouth of the river.

Evidently it would take some time for the situation to calm down and it was not until the end of 1873 that an independent engineer negotiated a plan. The Board normally raised revenue by imposing a rate on local property. Amongst their concerns was that this meant that the poorest in the town contributed disproportionately to the capital cost of improvements. One solution adopted elsewhere was to borrow money for the improvements and repay the principal over a long period. The interest and repayment were therefore spread over the period in which the system was in use. Littlehampton's Board however, did not at this time agree with borrowing.

The solution found was for the Duchy of Norfolk to buy a farm in a suitable area where a treatment plant and pumping station could be established. The Board would improve the drainage system. However, this plan was not operationalised. Discussions continued back and forth for several more years and extended to include the supply of fresh water.

Eventually it was agreed that the sewage system would be improved, with a new outfall at the river mouth, and that the Local Board would have a well dug to extract fresh water which would be distributed around the town with an additional system of underground pipes. In August 1880 the Duke of Norfolk laid the foundation stone of a water-tower in which water was pumped up from the well and stored for distribution. The new water system was estimated to cost more than £11,000, and the sewage system a further £11,000.

Illustration 11. Water Tower
(Littlehamapton Museum Collection)

In his speech the 15th Duke of Norfolk commented that both his father and grandfather had lived in Littlehampton and he himself had great affection for the town. An Eastbourne newspaper commented that the Duke seemed to be keen to make Littlehampton a fashionable resort to rival the Duke of Devonshire's efforts in Eastbourne[2]. It noted that there were some good, but small, hotels there and plenty of attractions, both scenic and artificial.

The new fort

From 1848 there was a period of significant uncertainty in France. The Bourbon monarchy was deposed and a new republic proclaimed. From 1850 Louis-Napoleon was named president and from 1852 he proclaimed France to be an empire with himself, as Napoleon III, the emperor. 1853 to 1856 was the period of the Crimean War. These unsettled times led to anxiety in Britain about security.

---

[2] In fact the Duchy of Norfolk also owned the centre of Sheffield and the 15th Duke arguably devoted much more time to the Yorkshire city, serving as mayor in the 1890s.

In 1852 the Royal Engineers surveyed the Sussex coast to assess 'the capabilities of the several forts for the national defence'. In the following year it was decided that a new fort should be built on the West bank of the Arun. This was to be the first 'Palmerston' fort which served as a prototype for others along the coast. The argument advanced was that a fort there could command a wide area of beach. The army report implied that the battery on the East bank should remain, but Goodwin (1985) says 'after 75years of guarding the entrance to the Arun the east bank battery was dismantled and sold off by the economical Board of Ordnance for use as a coastguard station' (p35).

Tenders were invited for a five-gun battery, which was built eventually by a London firm, in 1854. It was manned in 1855 by 40 men plus officers and NCOs of the Royal Artillery militia. A newspaper report of August 1855 notes that men from this force were also sent to help with the harvest. In 1859 it was decided to build an extra accommodation block measuring 50 feet by 20 feet.

To the west of the fort a firing range was established. We have not been able to determine exactly when, but the newspapers start to refer to companies of troops visiting for rifle practice later in the 1850s. In 1861 a member of the Local Board suggested the fact that the town has on its outskirts 'a military rifle practice ground and a garrison of soldiers' as one of the reasons to install gas lighting in the streets. At the 1862 annual meeting of the Sussex Yeomanry Association the Littlehampton range was described as 'one of the best ranges in the county' and 'a very excellent one'.

The newspapers report a succession of rifle competitions held at the 'government range' at Littlehampton. Normally a rifle range involves a protective wall behind the targets and a heavy layer of absorbent material, particularly sandbags, to stop the bullets going any further. Presumably the Littlehampton range involved the firing position being inland, so the soldiers would fire with their backs to the town and towards the sea. Reports say that the government had ranges also at Cuckfield and at Eastbourne.

The newspapers report a comment at a yeomanry dinner at the beginning of1889 that the Littlehampton contingent would now be disadvantaged by not having a local firing range. Later that year there are reports of a golf club being formed and a course being set out on the west bank of the Arun. The presumption is therefore that the government closed down its range in 1888. The Wikipedia page for the Littlehampton Fort (accessed in June 2022) says that it closed in 1873. Goodwin (1985) suggests that the last master gunner in charge was Mr Collinson who died while living at the fort in 1879. In January 1891 the guns were removed and the fort was finally dismantled as a defensive fortification. However, the 1899 Ordnance Survey map still shows the rifle range running back from the sea on the west side of the golf course.

A police presence

In 1857 the Littlehampton Board agreed that the town would be served by a police constable based at Wick. There had, of course, existed all sorts of mechanisms for enforcing the law for many hundred years. These included having watchmen or voluntary parish constables and a wide variety of other mechanisms such as the Bow Street Runners. Around 1800 various towns started to think about organising a more professional force and obtained acts of parliament in one or two cases. The most notable example is that of the Metropolitan Police, set up by Sir Robert Peel's act in 1829.

An 1839 Act (Rural Constabulary Act) provided a legal framework for counties to set up police forces if they wished. East Sussex took advantage of this and created a county force in 1840, but West Sussex did not[3]. Brighton had its own constabulary as did Arundel. Subsequently the 1856 County and Borough Police Act made it compulsory for professional forces to be created. West Sussex duly created a force in 1857. It was based at Petworth, and the first Chief Constable was Captain Montgomerie, a retired army officer who had had police experience in New South Wales.

---

[3] Sussex was formally considered to be divided into a 'Western Division' and an 'Eastern Division' until 1888 but the terms West Sussex and East Sussex were often used in the press. When Sussex – Western Division started up its police force this was known as the West Sussex police or West Sussex Constabulary.

Under the 1856 Act one quarter of the cost of the force was funded by the national government and the rest had to be raised from local taxation – the Police rate. A government inspector reported in 1858 that the West Sussex force had 72 officers and constables, but that the physical facilities where they were based required improvement. In 1862 the bench was asked to provide an extra constable for Littlehampton because there were lots of sailors in the streets and labourers building the railway. Eventually in 1874 the police superintendent was moved from Wick to an expanded Littlehampton police house.

Town lighting

The Local Board voted in August 1861 to install gas lighting in the town. One member argued that other towns that regularly received visitors had already installed lighting. Also, that the town, as a seaport, had many visiting seamen and also a garrison. He added that the gas works was extending its capacity and would be able to supply this. The Board agreed to install 30 lights and at its next session spent three hours walking around the town to determine where the lights should be placed.

The railway changes tracks

During the late 1850s there had been much discussion about the possibility of extending the Mid-Sussex line from Pulborough to Arundel and Ford. It was argued that this would reduce the rail journey from Portsmouth to Victoria by eleven miles. It was also proposed to then extend the line from Ford to Littlehampton. The case was argued in Parliament and the necessary legislation passed in March 1860, work started on the line in 1861. The improvement would mean building a new station at Arundel (and crossing the Arundel to Littlehampton road which ultimately proved quite difficult) as well as one at Littlehampton.

Some authors suggest that only with the siting of a station near the centre of Littlehampton did the railway become attractive to

Illustration 12. Railway wharf 1907
(Littlehampton Museum Collection)

passengers, but we disagree. The original station was two miles from the High Street, a distance that people thought nothing of walking at that time. Thomas Hardy as a youngster walked three miles a day to school and three back.

The *Brighton Gazette*, when Rustington parish church was refurbished, recommended its readers to visit the church. It noted that it was easily accessible from Angmering station. Anyone who has walked that distance will know that it is more than two miles and takes at least 30 minutes to complete on foot. In fact, the London, Brighton and South Coast Railway (LB&SCR) actively engaged in promoting events such as Littlehampton's regatta to encourage local use of the railway for leisure as soon as the first station was established in 1846.

The main reasons given for the branch line to Littlehampton were, however, to do with freight, not passengers. Initially freight was transferred between boats and railway at Ford, but LB&SCR wanted to do this at Littlehampton in the main harbour. In the event, they acquired about 1200 feet of river frontage on the East bank above the ferry crossing, and the freight line ran right onto the quay.

The photograph (Illustration 12 on previous page), shows what the railway quay looked like in 1907, and probably looked like from the time the new line was constructed. Terminus Road in 2022 runs between the quay and the railway station, but in 1863 when the railway quay was established, the road ended where the ferry came in, and the LB&SCR owned the land between the station and the quay. They ran a line along the quay and presumably others into a marshalling area and station.

Visitors to Littlehampton arriving by train in 2022 are surprised to find that if they leave the station at right-angles to the rails, they arrive in very little time at the river. The reason is that the 1863 installation was all about taking freight to the river, not taking passengers near to the High Street.

The LB&SCR made quite clear in their submissions to Parliament that the object of the exercise was to make it possible for steamers to come into Littlehampton harbour and cross the Channel to the Channel Islands and to Normandy. They included in submissions in 1862 a request to be empowered to operate steamships from Littlehampton to France – and also from Newhaven to Dieppe. Investors formed another company, the Littlehampton, Havre, and Honfleur Steam Ship Company, to operate across the Channel. They noted that it enabled travel between London and France in eight hours and saved at least 100 miles on the journey.

In a company report in January 1863 the LB&SCR directors commented: 'The Littlehampton branch of about two miles will give access to their excellent harbour which, it may be fully agreed, will obtain its due share of the traffic to the Channel Islands and the opposite coast of France.'

The main work involved building a railway line from Pulborough to Ford. In November 1861 the *Brighton Gazette* reported that the company had 200 men working on the line. At the same time the Harbour Commissioners had been prevailed upon to undertake large scale works to deepen the harbour so that it could accommodate the cross-channel steamers. In 1861 they succeeded in digging out a channel of three feet depth wide enough to accommodate one ship, with the promise this would be continued in 1862 to create a wider deep channel.

The original Brighton line had crossed the River Arun using a single track wooden bridge, with a section that could be retracted to allow boats to travel up river to Arundel. In the fifteen years following its opening it had been involved in at least two major train crashes, where the safety signalling had either been ignored or did not work and trains ran into each other. The Pulborough to Ford line project involved dismantling the old wooden bridge and replacing it with a double track iron structure. Nonetheless the bridge had still to be retractable to permit (increasingly rare) ship access to Arundel.

Illustration 13. Littlehampton railway station built 1863
(Greaves Collection)

The new Littlehampton station was opened in August 1863. The official opening involved a celebratory dinner attended by the Duke of Norfolk and the directors of the LB&SCR. The old Arundel and Littlehampton station at Lyminster was closed down within weeks. John Farrant (1972) notes that trains from London destined for Littlehampton were obliged to stop at Ford and then reverse up the two-mile branch line to Littlehampton. The line was run with steam engines until the 1930s, so the process of servicing the Littlehampton branch involved changing engines at some point.

In November 1863 the first steamer arrived from France, the *Vibourg*, with a mixed cargo of wine, brandy, fruit and eggs. The *Rouen* was next scheduled to leave Littlehampton for the Channel Islands and St Malo. In their 1863 annual report the LB&SCR directors were bullish, writing that they anticipated 'a considerable traffic between that harbour and the opposite coast of France'.

However, despite the great hopes of the railway company and others, this was the last great hurrah of the port. The harbour suffered as always from the perpetual creation by the tides and currents of a bar across the entrance, meaning that access was limited for larger boats to either side of high water. This was a nightmare for railway timetables. Although the harbour would be resuscitated briefly during the First World War, the cross-channel trade did not prosper.

According to Farrant (1972), the Littlehampton, Havre and Honfleur Steam Ship Company went bankrupt at the end of 1864. The court hearing which issued the winding up order in February 1865 implied that the company had used up nearly all its initial capital of £7,500 in 'setting-up' costs, leaving no working capital. It may be therefore a question of mismanagement, rather than lack of business. In any event the LB&SCR took over running the steamships.

Elleray (1991) says that the LB&SCR concentrated on the Honfleur service. They took the view that Le Havre was cut off from Lower Normandy by the River Seine, whereas Honfleur, on the south bank of the river, had good rail connections. They succeeded in running that profitably for some years, but there was competition from other railways, out of Southampton and Dover, to say nothing of LB&SCR's own Newhaven service. The 1871 advert from a newspaper published in Honfleur shows that at that time they were running two services a week using screw steamships, the *Rennes* and the *Ida*. Elleray reports that by the late 1870s the service had ceased to be profitable and the LB&SCR decided to close down its operation in Littlehampton harbour and concentrate on Newhaven.

He sees this period as the beginning of the decline of Littlehampton as a sea port. Aside from the problem of the harbour bar, sail was progressively giving way to steam as the source of power. Ships were being built out of iron and steel not wood, and were getting bigger. The combination of bigger ships and easy inland transport

Illustration 14. Advert for cross-Channel service 1971
(Peter Walton)

by rail meant the gradual disappearance of the coastal trade and the slow death of many a small seaport in the latter part of the nineteenth century. The Wey and Arun canal ceased trading as a commercial company in 1871, following the loss of canal traffic to the railway.

The passenger trains into Littlehampton station came via Ford. This involved the train either going backwards into Littlehampton having travelled from Brighton to Ford, or passengers changing trains at Ford and taking a smaller train the two miles back to Littlehampton. People began to be dissatisfied with this and eventually the LB&SCR built a loop line after Angmering that enabled the trains to go directly to Littlehampton without crossing the Arun. This modification was built in 1886 and opened in 1887. It remains in use today.

Expansion of the town

The 1890s was a decade of prosperity in Britain and it saw rapid expansion of economic activity. The 1881 census gave the population of Littlehampton as 3,932, which rose to 4,455 in the 1891 exercise. However, by 1901 the permanent population was recorded 5,954. Over twenty years the population had increased by 50%. The bigger population needed somewhere to live and very many houses were built in this period. The main areas of development were south of the High Street, including St Catherine's Road, Clifton Road and Bayford Road, and north of the railway station and High Street. Connections were built going east from Beach Road, including Fitzalan Road, Granville Road and Selborne Road, and South Terrace was extended westwards to the river. These would provide land for later developments. In effect the land between the old town centre and Beach Town began to be changed to urban use from farmland.

One sign of prosperity was that the Littlehampton Local Board felt sufficiently expansive as to build itself some council offices

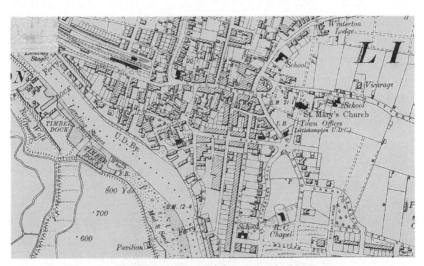

Illustration 15. Littlehampton in 1899
(Reproduced with the permission of the National Library of Scotland)

Illustration 16. Littlehampton town offices built 1893
(Peter Walton)

which opened in January 1894. These remain in use in 2022 as commercial offices at 41 Beach Road. The town council retains the adjacent garden, whose fountain was donated at the time the offices were built by the Constable family who operated a major brewery in the High Street in the nineteenth century. The basement of the building did at one time house a public convenience for women, even if we are told it now holds only file storage.

The town continued to expand rapidly, with its 1911 population reaching 8,351 – another 50% increase from 1901 – and, despite the First World War, reaching 11,412 in 1921 (although this includes 1,473 people living in Wick). This growth involved continued house-building and infill around the town. The area north of the town became much more densely built up, and houses started to appear along the new roads, between the old town and Beach Town.

Illustration 17. Littlehampton in 1913
(Reproduced with the permission of the National Library of Scotland)

Local Government

In the 1890s the government moved to another reform of local government. It had created county councils by the 1888 Local Government Act. West Sussex County Council came into being in 1889 and Littlehampton was represented on it by the chairman of the Local Board of Health. This represented a further move to organise democratic control of services such as roads, and move responsibility away from landowners and parish councils. Roads in particular were a continuing source of dispute but of considerable significance in economic development because of their impact on the cost and ease of transport.

In the first instance the Local Board of Health had taken some responsibility for roads from the parish council, but in Littlehampton this gave rise to years of discussion as to whether a particular road belonged to the Duchy of Norfolk or should be maintained by the Local Board, or anyone else. There was a particular anomaly with the road along the beach from Beach Town to Rustington. This had been built by the trustees of the Arun Ferry, supposedly as a feeder route for the ferry. However, by the 1880s the trustees no longer had the money to keep it in order, giving rise to years of acrimony and lawsuits involving Rustington Parish Council as well as Littlehampton.

The creation of the West Sussex Council then led to that body having some responsibility for maintaining roads. They negotiated with local boards, which could opt to retain responsibility for the roads but receive a grant towards upkeep.

The development of county councils was swiftly followed by the conversion of local boards of health into urban and rural district councils. The Littlehampton Board of Health ceased to exist on 31 December 1894, to be replaced by Littlehampton Urban District Council (LUDC). The Board had had six members whereas the LUDC had nine (although this was soon increased to twelve). The first chairman of the LUDC was Mr Joseph Robinson, the prominent ship-owner and businessman. All the members were people who had previously done terms on the Local Board, so there was in practice a good continuity.

Illustration 18. High Street c1900
(Greaves Collection)

The powers of the LUDC were wider than those of the Local Board and included control of planning and development. The LUDC would go on to facilitate the development of the resort activities by managing the beach and promenade and installing buildings such as a band stand, to provide entertainment during the season.

Wick

Under the reform of local government in the 1890s the parish of Lyminster to the north of Littlehampton had been put under the control of the newly-created East Preston Rural District Council. The parish included the sub-division of Wick, an expanding community which was largely a dormitory area whose inhabitants worked in Littlehampton. In effect Lyminster consisted of a built-up area of housing in its southern part and a rural, farming community in its northern part, adjacent to Arundel.

The first Wick problem to hit the East Preston RDC was an assessment that sanitation in the village was extremely poor and would have to be dealt with. The Lyminister rate-payers in the north of the parish were not keen, seeing themselves likely to be asked to pay for expensive services in the south of the parish which did not extend to the north, and indeed were unlikely to be needed in the rural north. East Preston RDC was similarly unenthusiastic about undertaking such a project, and the local authorities came up with the suggestion that Wick should be detached from Lyminster. They thought Wick could become part of Littlehampton and be attached to Littlehampton's now better-developed fresh water and sewage systems.

Littlehampton UDC were initially unenthusiastic also but in July 1897 a proposal was presented to the West Sussex County Council asking them to consider the transfer. The County Council appointed a committee which held a public inquiry into the idea. Nowadays such an inquiry could take months or even years, but in 1897 that simply consisted of the committee announcing a day

Illustration 19. Joseph Robinson, ship-owner and councillor
(Littlehampton Museum Collection)

on which they would receive representations at the LUDC offices. Lyminster suggested that Wick was urban in its nature and should more appropriately be administered by an Urban District Council than an essentially rural one.

In the end it was 1900 before the matter was settled and the county council issued an order that Wick should become part of Littlehampton from 29 September 1900. It is impossible to know what occurred in behind the scenes negotiations, but it appears that there was disagreement as to how much of Lyminister parish should be hived off; and, whether the school boards should retain their existing boundaries. It is likely that the 15th Duke of Norfolk supported the move and in practical terms he provided for fresh water to be piped from Crossbush to Wick – largely at the Duchy's expense.

The county council's order transferred 1400 acres to Littlehampton, consisting of all the land up to the Black Ditch. This was much in excess of the 600 acres originally proposed by East Preston RDC. It also provided for the school boards to be amalgamated and for a new parish of Wick to be recognised. East Preston RDC did not like this and protested to the Local Government Board (the national government agency with oversight of local government). Their protest was forwarded to West Sussex County Council who in turn ordered another public inquiry (actually the fifth on this issue). The Duke of Norfolk, Lyminster parish and Littlehampton UDC all supported the county council's order. Wick duly became part of Littlehampton – just in time for the 1901 census, where Wick was counted as having 1,413 inhabitants which were added to Littlehampton's 5,950.

Littlehampton UDC had agreed to augment their water supply by drilling in Warningcamp, but were slow to do this. The vicar of St Mary's, Rev Bebbington, was moved to write to the local paper in January 1901 warning that the town would run out of water in the summer of 1901, thanks to the council's lack of activity.

The Green and Foreshore Committee

The green and the foreshore belonged to the Duchy of Norfolk[4]. The green and the beach had long been used by the public and over time the Duchy had made attempts to build a seaside walk and some sea defences. However, as Littlehampton grew in size and started to be popular as a resort, after 1880, the Duchy found itself with problems controlling people's behaviour and use of this area.

Eventually, in 1898, the Duchy offered the LUDC an annual lease at the peppercorn rent of half a crown a year. This transferred the responsibility for managing the area to the Council which had more power, as for example with its ability to pass bye-laws, to manage the area and more interest on behalf of the town to develop it. In effect this put the principal resort asset of the town into the Council's hands, and opened up the possibility of development of its resort activity. The Duchy retained the obligation to build sea defences, and, as would be forcibly argued 25 years' later, as

---

[4] The sea bed below the low-water line belonged to the Duchy of Lancaster (the crown) and the beach between the low- and high-water lines was disputed between them

the freeholder of the whole of Littlehampton benefitted from the growth of the town and its increased prosperity.

From 1898 the Council was able to take steps to manage the shore and green and in effect to manage the resort for the first time. It created a committee, the Green and Foreshore Committee, whose responsibility it was to manage the resort facilities. In the early years it did this by designating various concessions, such as the right to rent deckchairs, or let bathing huts, or erect a stage on the green, and then renting these off season by season.

Illustration 20. Pop-up stage on the green c1905
(Greaves Collection)

These created revenue for the council but also gave the council the ability to regulate to an extent the quality and nature of the services provided. These included tea tents (concession 3/- a week), beach huts (1/- per hut per week), public meetings (e.g. the Salvation Army) and particularly two pitches for pop-up stages. These were usually taken by Harry Joseph (and his pierrots) and Dan Randall. The Blue Hungarian Band had a concession to play on the beach and also on Sunday nights at the band stand at the east end of the green. Other bands, especially military ones, played in the bandstand which the Council erected to the eastern end of the green during the week.

Over the years the LUDC made numerous attempts to improve the facilities, including building public lavatories, a new band stand at Banjo Road, given by the Duke, and in 1910 a public shelter near the Oyster Pond where people could take cover during bad weather and where shows could be staged in the evening. After the First World War they also erected shelters around Banjo Road so that people could listen to the bands playing in more comfort.

The Swing Bridge

A major innovation carried out by the LUDC was to replace the ferry across the Arun with a bridge. There was a significant part of the harbour above the bridge site, and so the bridge needed to be mobile to allow ships to pass by. The solution was a swing bridge, which could turn through 90 degrees to remove the obstruction to traffic. It was a toll bridge, and made a significant contribution to Littlehampton Council's revenues in the 1920s and 1930s, albeit against a growing tide of dissent that it acted as a restraint of trade. Today (2022) the site is occupied by a retractable footbridge.

By the latter part of the nineteenth century, it had become more obvious that a bridge was badly needed. In 1902 Neville Edwards, Chairman of the LUDC, along with George Groom and Rev Green, Vicar of Clymping, who were the prime promoters and a driving force for the bridge, had already put together ideas and costings for the type of bridge they thought would be needed to replace the chain ferry.

These were presented to the Council and in 1903 a special Bridge Committee was formed with Neville Edwards as chairman. The Council then decided they were ready to present them to the townspeople so accordingly, a prescribed grand public meeting took place on Friday 13th January 1903. It was a lively debate with speakers for and against the scheme. Following that meeting a referendum was arranged for the 31st January. Voting at the poll was not high but came out as following: For the bridge: 675; Against: 213.

Plans were taken to Parliament when a petition was put forward about the burden of cost which would be put on the LUDC. However, the Bill was passed mainly on the grounds that the barge was no longer safe to use. Royal Assent was granted on the 4th August 1905 which cleared the way for work on the new swing bridge to begin.

Tenders for the work were to be submitted to the Town Clerk, in the meantime in April engineers from Dando's made test borings of the river bed. It was decided because of soft ground on the west bank the opening section of the bridge should be on the east side of the river. The firm of Alfred Thorne & Sons of Westminster were given the contract. By May 1907 work was sufficiently ahead for the laying of the foundation stone which was performed by Henry 15th Duke of Norfolk.

Illustration 21. Opening of the toll bridge over the Arun May 1908
(Greaves Collection)

Work carried on at a pace and soon the bridge was ready for use. So, after nearly 100 years of planning and frustration, the grand official opening of Littlehampton's first bridge over the River Arun was carried out on the 27th May 1908 by the Duke of Norfolk. The day was declared a public holiday. A grand procession with school children, members of the public and armed forces lining the streets took place to celebrate this very festive occasion. It is estimated about 2000 children were given a ticket for a free tea party following the celebrations.

The LUDC had had to pay £8,500 in compensation to the former ferry company to persuade them to give up their rights to the crossing. The actual bridge cost another £16,500, but by 1910 the LUDC was reporting annual tolls of more than £1,800 and anticipating that it would soon become a net contributor to the town's finances. The replacement of the ferry by the bridge had, as forecast, resulted in a significant increase in traffic.

Cottage Hospital

In the nineteenth and early twentieth century there were no state hospitals. Those that existed were usually charitably funded. Towards the end of the nineteenth century, as Littlehampton expanded its population, the need started to be felt for the town to have its own hospital. Worthing had one, but there were delicacies about the extent to which it would take in patients from other areas. Littlehampton already had a nursing association which did sterling work, but they needed support. A public subscription was started, fund-raising events took place and in 1904 a cottage hospital was started in a house in Surrey Street. It had three beds for women, three for men and one for a child.

This was much-used but people quickly realised that the building was not well adapted to being a hospital, nor was it big enough. The Duke of Norfolk gave some land in Church Street, and more fund-raising followed. A purpose-built hospital was eventually opened in 1911.

Littlehampton and District Hospital.
Supported by Voluntary Contributions.

Illustration 22. Design for Cottage Hospital 1911
(Greaves Collection)

At the same time the LUDC was responsible for an isolation hospital situated in Wick. This was very small and the Council decided to replace it with a new building at Toddington. This was subject to constraints issued by national government which included that it should have a barbed wire fence to prevent people from approaching the hospital. Once again, the Duke of Norfolk provided the land, but was adamant that he did not want an external barbed wire fence. The Council finally solved this dilemma by building two fences with a hedge in-between them: an internal barbed wire fence, visible to the government inspectors, and an external fence visible to everyone else.

The Shelter Hall

During the first decade of the twentieth century the Council continued to operate its concessions on the Green, but the increasing holiday public started to point out that there was nowhere to go if the weather was bad. The LUDC decided therefore to build what was termed a Shelter Hall at the Western end of the green, near the windmill. This was intended to be a place where people could take their deckchairs if it was raining and was next to the No 1 pitch for a pop-up stage.

The Shelter Hall itself had a stage and two dressing rooms and was made available to the concessionaire of the no 1 pitch in the evenings. Although the hall was intended to have free access, of course the concert party performers eyed it with interest as an ideal place to perform on wet afternoons. The Shelter Hall remained a bone of contention from its inception between those who wanted it to stage performances and those who insisted it was for free public use.

This was partly alleviated after the war, when shelters were built round the bandstand, since these offered much more space, at which time, the Shelter Hall started to be referred to as the "Pavilion on the Green".

Death of the Duke of Norfolk

The 15th Duke of Norfolk had acceded to the title at the age of thirteen in 1860 and eventually died in February 1917. His tenure of the dukedom had coincided with the development of Littlehampton as a seaside resort, and indeed he had been generous throughout in terms of encouraging development and giving both land and money to the town for that purpose. Amongst other things he had given land for the library, the hospital, the sports ground and a recreation park in Maltravers Road, as well as for the pumping station at Warningcamp. The chairman of the Council described him as having been 'a true friend' of Littlehampton.

During a large part of his time, his Estate manager for Little-hampton had been Lt Col Mostyn. It was a sad coincidence that Lt Col Mostyn died in 1916, so that the two men who had been most involved in dealing with the estate and growing Littlehampton died within months of each other. This signalled a major change in relations between the Estate Office and the Council. The 16th Duke was only six years' old in 1917. The 15th Duke's first wife had died in 1887 and their son had died in 1902; the 16th Duke was the fruit of a late second marriage.

The 16th Duke could make no decision until he was 21 years old; the estate being administered by trustees, including his mother, the 15th Duchess of Norfolk. The dukedom had last changed hands nearly 60 years previously and had benefitted from the growth of the UK economy and the absence of taxation. However, the social reforms of the early twentieth century followed by the First World War saw the introduction of swingeing death duties and severe increases in the rates of income tax.

These changes created havoc with landed fortunes, some of which never recovered. It is likely that the death of the 15th Duke actually precipitated a financial crisis for the Duchy and a change in attitudes. It was reported in the *Littlehampton Gazette* in April 1924, that the Duchess of Norfolk had wanted to rent out Arundel Castle.

One manifestation of the change was that in October 1923 the Estate Office told Littlehampton Council that the annual lease of the green and foreshore for half a crown (12½p) would not be renewed. A new 10-year lease would be available at a rental of £300 a year. The Council was completely taken by surprise: had they not been encouraged to spend ratepayers' money on developing the Green? Did the Duchy not benefit as the freeholder of the town? The chairman declared that such a demand was morally reprehensible, but the Duchy was unmoved, and the Council had to pay. It took the view that it was very much in the interests of the ratepayers to control the green and the beach, so they gritted their collective teeth and paid.

Women's rights

The first (partial) enfranchisement of women took place in 1918 and after that, women in Littlehampton started to play a more prominent role. Mary Neal was appointed a magistrate in 1925 and sat on the bench regularly. In the same year Mrs Lilian Drummond-Murray was elected to the Littlehampton Urban District Council, the first woman to sit on the council.

Museum

Littlehampton included a historical society, called the Nature and Archaeology Society, which lobbied the Council to add a museum to the library. The proposal was to build on to the library to create a separate but connected museum, which would be run by volunteers. The Council was prepared to entertain this and eventually this was funded half by a donation from estate of Alan Thompson (a former chairman of the LUDC who had left money for the improvement of Littlehampton) and the rest by the Council. John Ede Butt donated some exhibition cases. The museum was formally opened on 30th May 1928 (*Littlehampton Gazette*).

The coming of Butlin

In 1932, the whole nature of the resort was changed by a decision of the Duchy of Norfolk. They sold the Windmill site (including the Casino) to Billy Butlin who established an amusement park around the windmill. It opened with temporary buildings, taking in fact several years to settle down. The sale of the site upset the Council, who believed that they were in negotiation to buy it, and its acquisition by Billy Butlin changed the nature of what Littlehampton was offering the visitor.

The vociferous Local Government Electors' Association (which changed its name to the Ratepayers' Association later) was outraged because it felt that Butlin's amusement park attracted just the sort of day-trippers which they did not want. It inveighed against the coachloads of Sunday trippers who they said brought their own food and drink, created a big nuisance and then left behind their rubbish and spent no money in the town. They demanded that the Council clamped

Illustration 23.
Advert for Butlin's amusement park

down on Butlin, stopped the coaches coming to Littlehampton, and preserved the tranquil nature of the resort which was what attracted those who wanted to spend their holidays there.

In fact, Littlehampton as a resort had served two different markets since the arrival of the railway: the day-tripper, and the holiday-maker spending several days or even weeks in the town. This was a dilemma for all seaside resorts. The day-tripper wants to bathe, use the beach, eventually watch daytime entertainments, and to be able to buy food and drink, and then goes home in the evening. The longer term holiday-maker wants possibly all of these but also evening entertainment and accommodation as well as food. While paid holidays started to be a feature of employment from the end of the nineteenth century, they were not a legal right until 1938. As a consequence, the holiday-maker tended to be more middle and upper class.

Littlehampton Urban District Council responded to the ratepayers by pointing out that most day-trippers were well-behaved, that the Council had no powers to stop them coming, and they should be welcomed. Of course, the Council did have planning powers and some influence over the music licence, and could have done more to restrain the amusement park. However, the Council was ambivalent. In 1931 it had rented part of the area next to the Windmill for a Dodgems amusement itself.

Also Butlin was extremely careful about how he handled the Littlehampton community. He offered the use of his park for charity events in June and September, supporting the parish church, the scouts, the hospital and other local interests. He complied immediately with any Council requirement, and he advertised Littlehampton widely. Indeed, a few years later, one councillor suggested, only half joking, that the Council should cancel its advertising budget because Butlin did it more effectively.

We are of the view that the area in the corner between the river and the sea was at that time split into two sites (see map p83)

support the temporary Red Cross Hospital in Fitzalan Road and other activities connected to the war. However, considerable though the effort was, all was wound down quickly at the end of the war and 1919 saw the resumption of the previous social life.

Concert halls and theatres

We have found no reference to Elleray's barn-theatre in the High Street after 1848, other than in Ayles, Gray and Redman (1996) who reproduce a photograph of the old barn advertising 'animated pictures'. They note that the barn was demolished in 1897. Once the Congregational Church built its Lecture Hall in 1865, this became the most regularly cited venue for all sorts of events, ranging from public lectures and political hustings through to concerts and fund-raising events for various local causes. The other popular venue in the 1870s was the National Schools in East Street, which were also used for meetings of the Local Board of Health and of course the Schools Board. St Mary's had a church hall which was demolished in 1871.

A break-away Episcopalian Reform church dedicated to St Saviour was built in New Road in 1878. The church shortly after built an adjoining church hall. St. Saviour's was of course outside the Church of England structure (and indeed the Bishop of Chichester delivered dire warnings about anyone worshipping there when it was opened) and depended on voluntary contributions. The incumbent fell ill (he died in August 1890) so an assistant was appointed. However, disagreements arose and the congregation broke up. The church was sold in June 1890 and started to be used as a concert venue, called the Victoria Hall. Confusingly the church hall next door was re-named St Mary's Hall and was also used for public events.

The Victoria Hall was the subject of great controversy in 1893 when 'Professor' Pelham applied to the Arundel magistrates for a theatrical licence for the two halls. Pelham was a well-known Littlehampton character who was an accomplished entertainer as a ventriloquist and a magician, as well as an experienced pleasure boat operator and coxswain of the Littlehampton lifeboat.

Charles Pelham appears In Kelly's Directory as living in Pier Road. Assuming there was only one Charles Pelham in Littlehampton, he also had a licence to rent bathing machines on the beach. He seems to have been a willing entrepreneur in serving Littlehampton's resort trade with boat trips for visitors, bathing and theatrical entertainments.

He often appeared as a performer in local fund-raiser entertainments and now seemed to want to become a theatre manager and impresario. He proposed making the Victoria Hall a theatre; this included opening up a new stage entrance to the hall and connecting it to St Mary's Hall, which would be used as dressing rooms for the performers.

When the matter was put to the bench, there was strong opposition from William Harvey, the shipbuilder and member of the Local Board, who argued that the local residents had built their houses close to a church and did not want the church to

Illustration 36. Handbill advertising Professor Pelham

become a centre for noise and nuisance. He referred to the building always as St Saviour's, rather than the Victoria Hall. He did not think it appropriate to convert a consecrated building into a place of entertainment. He did not object to Littlehampton having a theatre, but it should not be in a residential street.

In a subsequent interview with the *West Sussex County Times* (25th March 1893) it also became clear that when St Saviour's was built, Harvey's sister had paid for a stained-glass window to be installed in the church, and was upset at this being incorporated into a theatre.

The magistrates refused to make a decision without hearing from the Littlehampton Local Board. The Board duly considered the question at its next meeting, but chairman John Whitehead in turn refused to debate it. He ruled that the Board was not empowered to grant theatrical licences and could not give an opinion. It noted only that its surveyor had reviewed the proposed alterations and had no objections on planning grounds.

The Littlehampton Ratepayers' Association[6] held a noisy meeting at which it expressed its support for the proposed theatre, while W B Harvey canvassed more support from residents in the area. The application came back to the magistrates and this time the licence was awarded. At the hearing Mr Harvey again voiced his objections to a theatre replacing a church and noted that it should not be on consecrated ground. One of the magistrates countered that the land had been leased and that precluded consecration.

Another resident, Mr Sida, reported that he had been to Worthing and Bognor and seen that no houses were built anywhere near the theatres in those towns. The chairman of the magistrates suggested it would be better that the building had a theatrical licence because then it would be subject to strict controls on its opening whereas currently it could stay open all hours.

---

[6] This organisation disappeared before the First World War. However a new body, the Local Government Electors Association, was formed in the 1920s and subsequently changed its name to the Ratepayers' Association.

The license was granted by the magistrates subject to it applying to the Victoria Hall and St Mary's Hall together and various alterations being made to improve access. They also specified that Mr Harvey should be allowed to remove the stained-glass window and replace it with a plain one.

The *West Sussex County Times* welcomed this as Littlehampton's first theatre, noting that there was otherwise nothing for visitors to do if the weather was poor. It suggested that without entertainment visitors would be inclined to move to the adjacent resorts with artificial facilities in addition to the natural ones.

However, even if the Victoria Hall had a theatrical license, it would be somewhat generous to call it a proper theatre. To the enthusiast a theatre would normally have a raked auditorium (the floor sloping upwards towards the back of the auditorium to improve sight lines) and a raked stage (the stage sloping up towards the back wall for the same reason); it would have at least a circle (also raked) and the stage would have a fly tower (the scenery could be held on ropes above the stage and be lowered in as required). As far as we know, Littlehampton has sadly never had such a theatre. The Victoria Hall would have had a flat floor and a raised flat stage, and would have been called a pavilion or assembly room in some resorts.

The question of a theatre for the town was a vexed one throughout this period. On the one hand, many people thought it was a necessary facility for a respectable sea-side resort. On the other, it was doubtful if anyone could make it pay consistently. Other than by Charles Pelham, the nettle seems never to have been grasped. In the event, Mr Pelham's venture does not seem to have lasted for long. The former church building was sold to the local Methodist congregation in 1896.

One of the difficulties of analysing Littlehampton's entertainment capacity is the fact that buildings frequently changed names over their lives, even if their use did not necessarily change. The hall attached to St Saviour's was known as St Mary's Hall for a while, even if it was not attached to St Mary's church, and when there had earlier been a similarly named hall that was part of that church.

In this connection there are numerous mentions of the Jubilee Hall, also in New Road. Some people suggest that this was the same building as either St Mary's Hall or the Victoria Hall. However, the Victoria County History says (p164) that 'Assembly Rooms in New Road, later called the Victoria Hall, were erected to commemorate Queen Victoria's Jubilee in 1887'.

Illustration 37. Terminus Hotel
(Greaves Collection)

The Terminus Hotel also had a concert hall which appears occasionally in the newspapers as having 'smoking concerts' (the Terminus Hotel was presumably also able to sell alcoholic drinks, which the other venues could not). Kelly's Directory for 1911 describes this as being used for theatrical entertainments and banquets and being capable of seating 500 people. The Victoria County History describes the Terminus Hall as occupying a site opposite the railway station (also the site of the Terminus Hotel) and being able to seat about 500 people. It says it created a roller-skating rink in 1909 which in turn later became a cinema.

Elleray (2006) does not mention the Terminus Hall in his gazetteer of Littlehampton theatres, but it is clear from the newspapers that as the town grew in size and in popularity as a resort between 1890 and 1914, the Terminus Hall was promoted more and more as a theatre. In particular a lessee called Wally Rice seems to have been particularly active before the First World War in promoting all sorts of entertainments, including plays and cinematic representations

First boom period

The twenty-five years before the start of the First World War were a boom period for Littlehampton as a middle-class resort, even if the town had yet to start thinking of itself as a resort, rather than a dwindling port. Pelham's conversion of St Saviour's is indicative of the visitor population reaching a size where there was a market for such entertainments. He staged two shows a week (i.e. playing for three days each), usually with visiting artists or companies.

However, there was a geographical split in the provision of entertainment between the beach area and the town centre. In many resorts the seaside entertainment is to be found on the promenade, just off the beach. But in Littlehampton this area was set aside for the green, and beyond that were only houses and hotels. Arguably there were two entertainments streams: one on the green, performing during the day and aimed at families on the beach, and the other in the town, providing evening entertainment.

Once the Littlehampton Urban District Council (LUDC) leased the green and foreshore from the Duchy of Norfolk (1898), it set up its Green and Foreshore Committee to control entertainment and commercial activity in that area. For the most part it offered concessions to independent operators who paid a rent for a licence to trade at that time. The council also built a bandstand at the eastern end of the green, where the Victoria County History says that bands played from 1903. The Duke of Norfolk provided a new bandstand in 1913 in Banjo Road.

The LUDC either rented a concession to a band (for example the Blue Hungarian Band paid 1/- per night to play on Sunday evenings) or itself engaged bands to play during the summer, with collections taken from people listening in nearby deckchairs. The Duke of Norfolk for a number of seasons offered the services of the band of the fourth battalion of the Royal Sussex Regiment, provided at his expense.

At the beach regular performers like Harry Joseph and his concert party (from 1892) and Dan Randall and then later Fred Spencer (from 1914) would erect a pop-up stage on the green, with people watching from deck-chairs and paying in to a collection, as compared to the Victoria Hall where people bought tickets and had formal seats in the normal way. Carolyn Brown (1991) says that Harry Joseph also appeared at the Victoria Hall. The council in the early years licensed two 'pitches' on the green, of which one was regularly taken by Harry Joseph for his 'pagoda' stage. Dan Randall was often the concessionaire of the second. They paid £60 a season each.

Illustration 38. Fred Spencer
(Littlehampton Museum Collection)

From 1910 there was a fairly rapid expansion of the entertainment provision, with moves to build indoor facilities and the arrival of film. The Council became more proactive and also attempted to keep more revenue for itself. At first, there was some concern

Illustration 39. Bandstand and Shelter Hall c1915
(Greaves Collection)

that there was nowhere for people to go if the weather was unpleasant, so in 1910 the council built a public shelter on the green, not far from the oyster pond.

The shelter, known at this time as the Shelter Hall, had a stage. While people had free access during the day, the Council provided that the shelter could be used for an entertainment after 6pm. In 1910 the Council also asked for competitive tenders for the two concessions to stage shows in the green. Dan Randall won pitch no 1 with a bid of £130 (Harry Joseph bid £120). Pitch No 1 carried with it the right to use the public shelter in the evening. Harry Joseph had to be content with Pitch No 2, for which he paid £100.

The pitches had become more sophisticated, with Harry Joseph erecting an awning over his to protect the audience. This however attracted the ire of the residents in South Terrace. They held their properties on long leases from the Duchy of Norfolk, which in turn guaranteed that the green in front of the buildings would be kept free of disturbance. Lt Col Mostyn, the estate manager, was called in and established that they were not concerned about the actual shows, but only the awning.

The issue rumbled on, with suggestions that the holder of the no 2, easterly pitch could use the local shelter in the evenings. However, by 1913 the no 2 pitch had disappeared and only the no 1 pitch was available, and won by Harry Joseph, who also operated the Kursaal for the first time that year. A rather sad unintended consequence was an appeal from a Derby cinema manager for funds to help pay for Dan Randall's stay in a mental hospital. The appeal cited Randall's sixteen years working in Littlehampton and said his failure to win a pitch had caused a breakdown.

It seems that Harry Joseph was not too happy with the arrangements because he opened a new theatre, the Kursaal in 1913. The Kursaal was in the area between the oyster pond and the old battery and could show films as well as stage shows. However, Harry Joseph was to be found complaining at the end of 1913 that his show on the no 1 pitch had not done well and asking for his agreed rent of £160 to be reduced to £80. He complained that his pitch had been disturbed by works relating to the drainage system during the summer, but the town councillors noted that he was competing with himself at the Kursaal.

Eventually (June 1914), the LUDC took Joseph to court for the balance of his 1913 fee. Joseph argued that his business had suffered greatly because of works going on near the site in connection with the sewage system. He asserted that his audience had to walk through mud, and the performances were often drowned out by the movement of heavy machinery. The council rejected his plea, arguing that he had tendered £160 for the site, without pre-conditions. The court found for the LUDC, and that does appear to be the last time Joseph did any theatrical business with the Council (although in the 1920s he rented a kiosk by the beach to sell a game he had invented).

Harry Joseph seems to have operated as a show business entrepreneur, based on Littlehampton. He told the court that he had provided concerts on the sea front for the last 12 years and was a popular character in the locality as a performer. The season

Illustration 40. Harry Joseph's Pierrots
(Littlehampton Museum Collection)

at Littlehampton usually lasted about 16 weeks and during the rest of the year it was pantomimes, tours or no work. He also appeared often in Worthing. Later he seems to have produced pantomimes and other entertainments for other promoters in different parts of the country. He must have had a production office in Littlehampton, and can be found advertising for staff in the local papers. He was the nearest thing the town had to its own impresario.

Developments in town

The boom in entertainment was also manifest in the rapid construction of what was originally described as a skating rink on Church Street, near St Mary's church. This was first called the Olympic Hall, and featured a maple floor for roller-skating and an extension outside with a partition that could be opened to permit skaters to continue to the outside if they wanted to. The operation was financed by what the newspapers called a 'local syndicate', chaired by Mr Frank Nye, a Littlehampton councillor and businessman, and run by a professional manager brought down from London.

At the opening, in March 1910, the chairman of the council welcomed the new building, commenting that the town needed an indoor entertainment facility, and especially one so much bigger than the others, which would permit larger gatherings. Mr Nye agreed that while the exterior was not 'a thing of beauty', it had been designed with a view to permitting the staging of theatrical events as well, and on a scale that other venues could not provide. When it was operating as a cinema after the war, its capacity was given as 760 seats.

The management organised a series of events such as fancy-dress balls and carnivals on skates to attract custom. Such was the interest created that even the Duchess of Norfolk spent an afternoon there. Nonetheless, the hall was provided with a temporary stage and could host concerts and theatrical entertainments. By the summer of 1911 the Olympic was featuring visiting theatrical entertainments that performed just for one or two nights and moved on.

The Terminus Hall was used solely as a cinema that season, and was now run by a film enthusiast, a Desmond Holderness, in partnership with a local man, Charles Shepherd. His film programme changed twice a week. However, he was a film maker as well as exhibitor and his programme often featured short films of local events. He shot these and they were on the screen in two or three days. By 1912 the Olympic Hall was also showing films regularly out of season as well as operating in season as a theatre, and all year round as a skating rink. Such was the enthusiasm for skating that a 'rink hockey' club was formed which competed with similar groups from Worthing, Chichester and Bognor.

However, in 1913 Frank Nye sold up and left Littlehampton. No explanation is given in the newspapers, but he is reported to have spent fifteen years in Littlehampton where he traded successfully, eventually opening several branches of his shop. The 1911 Kelly's directory shows him as operating dairies in New Road, Beach Road and Cornwall Road. He served as a member of the council for three years and was the first chairman of the Littlehampton Traders' Association. He was the originator of the Olympic Hall syndicate and had a number of side interests including the football club and the Philharmonic Society. He was a supporter of the Congregational church.

Late in 1913, several months after his departure, the Olympic Hall was acquired by Mr Shepherd and Mr Holderness, of the Electric Picture Palace. They re-named the building the Empire Cinema and installed the latest projection equipment. There were some concerns that skating would have to stop, but a policy of mixed use was continued, with the building available for skating three times a week, and presenting films and live theatre as well.

Illustration 41 Olympic Hall later Empire then Palladium Cinema (Greaves Collection))

Cinemas

Films started to be shown in the UK towards the end of the nineteenth century, but it took several decades before the industry settled into its formula (which disappeared again in the 1970s) of a programme consisting of two 90-minute features shown in an ornate, purpose-built cinema. In the early years commercial films were short, and were often shown in theatres. Variety theatres especially were happy to install equipment and show a ten-minute film in the middle of a programme of variety acts. At some resorts enterprising managers would erect marquees and show films on the beach. For several years films were shown regularly by touring cinema shows in special halls and also in buildings with other uses, as was probably the case at the old barn theatre.

However, projecting those early films was technically challenging. The projector would only take a reel lasting ten minutes, so normally you would need to install two projectors with the ability to switch between them every ten minutes. The life of a projectionist was not one of leisure watching films, but rather running from one projector to another to take off the old reel, re-wind it ready for the next performance and fit the new reel - while keeping them all in the right order.

The film carried cue marks in the top right-hand corner of the screen. These gave first a ten-second warning, at which the projectionist should start the leader running on the second projector, and then at the second cue, open up the blind in front of the second projector and close the first. On screen the picture would shift either to a new scene, or a different camera angle on a continuing scene, so that the change of projectors was not apparent to the audience.

The other major problem was the intensity of the light source. The light had to project a large image through several hundred feet, and an electric filament could not produce the required intensity. The projectors, up to and including the 1970s, used carbon arc lights. These produced an intense light by passing a very high voltage current across two carbon terminals. The carbon rods used to make the light burned down systematically and another vital part of the projectionist's job was to advance them together as they were consumed, This required constant attention, interspersed with occasional panics if a rod had been damaged before installation and a piece dropped off in mid-reel.

The actual material used for the film itself was highly flammable and was capable of spontaneous combustion. The carbon-arc light developed a very high temperature and therefore, if the film became stuck in the gate where light was passed through it, it could easily burn. Fire was a significant hazard, and potentially life-threatening, given the number of people present in a confined space.

In effect, anyone wishing to start showing films needed a substantial investment in equipment plus a high-power electricity source well beyond what was used domestically, as well as trained staff to run the projection.

The Terminus Hall started to show occasional films in 1909, alongside a major live theatre activity. However, these were so popular that by 1911 it had been reconfigured as the Electric Picture Palace. It was unusual in having a screen made of plaster, and its own generator to develop a powerful enough current to operate the carbon-arc lamps. However, disaster struck in August 1914 when a fire in one of the projectors soon spread to the rest of the theatre, despite the best attentions of the fire brigade. Since Shepherd and Holderness now controlled the Empire as well, they simply concentrated their programme there. It may have been a relief to them in that the outbreak of war had seriously upset the distribution of films.

According to Eyles, Gray and Readman (1996) the cinema was nonetheless swiftly restored and re-opened in September 1914, with added safety features to protect the auditorium from any possible fire in the 'lantern room'. However, Eyles, Grey and Readman (1996) point out that in 1915 the licence was in the name of Maurice Mansbridge, reverting to Shepherd in 1924. In 1930 the Shepherd family sold the Electric Picture Palace to an established cinema partnership (Filer and Shinebaum). The following year it was refurbished, a sound system was installed and it re-opened in March 1931 as the Regent. It was the smallest of the Littlehampton cinemas, with only 650 seats, and was the first to stop operating as a cinema, in 1960. It was used for bingo for a while but the building was used for storage after 1974.

The Palladium

Roller-skating was a popular pastime in 1910 when the Olympic Hall was built but the building was capable of being used as a theatre. When it was taken over by Charles Shepherd and Desmond Holderness in 1913, it continued to operate as a multifunctional building with some roller-skating, films, live theatre and occasional concerts. Desmond Holderness disappeared from the management in about 1914, probably to join up. In 1916 it was taken over by Harry Joseph, who changed its name to the Palladium. Joseph continued through the war but appears to have given up in 1920.

The cinema continued to be owned by the Shepherd family until they sold out in 1930 to the Filer and Shinebaum partnership who immediately installed a sound system. Littlehampton had its first 'talkies'. It closed in 1986 – its presence is reflected only in the name of the *Amenic Court* block of flats on the site today.

In fact, when Harry Joseph gave up the Palladium, he filed for bankruptcy and in the court hearings (February 1922) he cited the Palladium as the source of his troubles. He told the court that when he acquired the premises 'it was quite devoid of fittings or furniture, even the handles of the doors had been removed.' He added that he had lost money on the place in 1916, 1917 and 1918; he said he had lost about £800 overall. Mr Joseph was resident in Littlehampton, his wife owned the

Illustration 42. Harry Joseph (Littlehampton Museum Collection)

Littlehampton 1800 to 1940

Kursaal, and after the bankruptcy he continued to work in the entertainment sector until his death in 1932.

During the war the town remained quite busy as a resort, and its entertainment offering continued. The outbreak of war caused people in August 1914 to cancel and stay at home, but even by September the holiday business was back (at that time the season ran to the beginning of October). The Council noted a drop of about 20%-25% in bridge tolls which would be consistent with a fall in traffic. However, in 1915 the town was reporting that all accommodation was pretty well full. The major difference was that the railway company was no longer operating any excursion trains, so there was a major drop in day visitors.

Entertainment was hit in a number of ways – the Blue Hungarian Band for example returned to Austria in August 1914, and other bands and pierrot troupes lost young performers who volunteered for the services. Nonetheless Fred Spencer arrived on the scene and mounted his concert party on the green, while Harry Joseph was at the Kursaal (which he re-named the Casino, supposedly because of a desire to distance himself from a German-sounding name).

The Council, though, took the view that they should not be providing bands during the war. Although this was contested by those who said that the town should do its best to entertain so that people would come back after the war. The popular view was that many people took holidays on the South coast during the war who would normally have gone elsewhere. It was 1917 before the Council engaged a band – and then for only six weeks.

After the war – a professional resort

As is apparent, the First World War brought to an end the informal expansion of the resort and the services intended to entertain the visitor. There was the inevitable shortage of manpower, significant inflation (an accumulated 100% from 1914

124

out the replacement of the wooden piles for a cost of £15,000, and proposed that this should be paid for in part by West Sussex County Council and the LUDC, with the neighbouring councils of Arundel and East Preston also making a small contribution. The argument they advanced was that if the mouth of the Arun collapsed, it would be not only Littlehampton but also the Arun Valley which would suffer.

The various authorities concerned had multiple meetings to discuss different configurations of a possible future Harbour authority. At one point the West Sussex County Council was going to take 50% of the future authority, but Worthing disputed this, arguing that they paid for their own sea defences and did not see why Littlehampton could not do the same. A different configuration then drew objections from Arundel but agreement was finally reached with Littlehampton the biggest contributor.

A bill to re-configure the authority was put before Parliament and finally succeeded in creating a Harbour Board in 1927 whose members were the representatives of the various bodies now responsible for funding it. A major reconstruction plan costing £75,000 was embarked upon, with the bonus that half of this would be paid by the Ministry of Transport. A further bonus was that port trade started to pick up a bit as well.

The work was completed by 1930, but not before the Harbour Board had had a row with the London Brighton and South Coast Railway. A 1929 bill sponsored by the railway company and addressing modernisation (electrification was just starting) proposed to replace the 'sliding bridge' at Ford with a permanent one. Both the Harbour Board and Arundel council were up in arms, and yachts were sent up and down the river to force the bridge to open. The railway company was reminded that it had a statutory duty to open the bridge with a delay of no more than 20 minutes. The bill was amended to delete the offending clause[5].

---

[5] Nonetheless, as discussed in the infrastructure chapter above, the Harbour Board finally gave in and in 1938 the bridge was replaced with a permanent one to allow electrification to proceed.

Although the harbour had been at its lowest point just after the war – described as 'virtually derelict' – as time went by, and particularly once refurbishment started, shipping began to revive a little. One problem that the Harbour Board faced was that it did not directly control any wharves. In particular the railway company still owned a 900-foot stretch on the East Bank that it did not use any more. Even worse, it was covered in sidings, and could not be used for transfer from ship to lorry. In a sense the harbour was a victim of its own history, and it would take years to unwind and modernise.

Traditional occupations

Alongside the increase in traffic and trade, smuggling became rife among the river people in the nineteenth century. Although a hazardous and sometimes dangerous pursuit – in 1835 a smuggler was reported drowned in the Arun after a pursuit by the coastguards – organised smuggling along the coast took place and many local families were involved in some way or the other. Privateers raided ships leaving the harbour and by the eighteenth-century, Sussex newspapers were reporting "tonnes of contraband" gin, cognac, rum, tea and lace being seized by the coastguards. Some smugglers were carrying arms. Smuggling began to fade as the fiscal and economic environment changed as well as the effectiveness of coastal blockades and the coastguards improved.

Littlehampton was a base for coastguard operations, and in the first half of the century many cases going through the courts talked of false compartments on boats landing at Littlehampton, or rowing boats putting in to beaches along the coast. There continued to be cases in front of the Arundel magistrates until about 1870, but these had tailed off after about 1850. To the current times people insist that there are blocked up passages leading up from the river and connecting the pubs between the river and the High Street to distribute smuggled tobacco

Illustration 31. Fishermen in Pier Road 1927
(Greaves Collection)

and spirits. It should be remembered though that the terrain had previously been river bed, and it is not clear how viable subterranean passages would have been.

There were fishermen based at Littlehampton; tradition has it that they used what is now Pier Road alongside the river but was known as 'Mussel Row'. There were oyster beds along the coast which attracted specialist dredging oyster catchers from places such as Brightlingsea and Colchester. The pond just back from the river bank and north of the east bank gun battery was constructed to enable fishermen to keep their oysters fresh until they were sold. This is currently known as the Oyster Pond, even if it now serves as a base for model sailing boats and boats for children.

Ships and ship building

There has generally been quite a close connection between the thriving ship-building industry of nineteenth century Littlehampton and ship operations. Sometimes this has been a family connection but it could also be a natural extension from the one to the other. For example, Henry Harvey was a major ship-builder but also retained part-ownership on occasions with a ship operator. The Isemonger brothers both built ships and operated them.

Initially ship-building took place only on the East bank of the river, but the start of the ferry in 1825 opened up the west bank. First one of the Ollivers and then Henry Harvey established yards there which in the twentieth century produced yachts and large motor boats.

Thomas Isemonger and his brother Richard had shipyards on the east bank near the ferry. Thomas was a shipbuilder and Harbour Commissioner and is mentioned as building sloops for the Royal Navy in 1770. Richard Isemonger was Assistant Astronomer on HM Barque 'Pagoda' on a successful expedition to Antarctica in 1875. The Isemonger's owned much of the property in River Road. Richard Isemonger used the brig "Oeconomy" and schooner "Littlehampton" in the timber and coal business. In about 1816 the Isemongers also had a ropeworks (ropery) in Oakum Row in East Street. When demolished the bricks were used to build houses in Duke Street, but part of the boundary wall is still in place.

John Corney and Jeffrey Carver established a shipyard in 1804 along Fisherman's Quay and Town Quay, building ocean-going sailing ships. They launched two 18-gun sloops in 1851. Edward Corney was a sailmaker. This site was later divided into three, Butts, Dukes and Paines. The Port of Arundel Commissioners subsequently made this a public launching and standing for boats

Stephen Diddlesfold Olliver established a ship repair yard, sawmill, rope works and smithy in 1837 on the west bank, the first to do so. Olliver preferred the sawmill side of the business and gained a good reputation for the standard of timber supplied. Some of the wood was used to build the Aldershot Barracks. After leasing part of the site to Henry Harvey, Olliver concentrated on the rope works. Unfortunately, in 1868 the ropery burnt down and was never replaced. However, the road leading to west beach and the golf course has retained the name of Rope Walk. Richard Isemonger also established a site on the west bank next to Stephen Olliver.

Henry Harvey, a master craftsman and shipbuilder, came to Littlehampton from Rye in 1846 and took a lease on Olliver's yard on the west bank where he established the Clymping shipyard 1846-1921. Under his management the yard gained a good reputation for finely built ocean-going vessels of 500/600 tonnes until 1880s when the demand for large sail-ships declined and they moved into building smaller ketch rigged barges, the last one in 1919.

The Harveys had a talent for making the launch of each hull into a big event. They usually contrived to launch at least one at each regatta held on the river. The most notable difficulty with the launches were that if the hull came too quickly down the slipway, there was the risk that it would continue right across the river and hit the opposite bank. They had to deploy boats in the river to restrain each newly-launched hull. Fitting out was often done in other places, such as Portsmouth.

Illustration 32. Harvey's yard
(Littlehampton Museum Collection)

Henry died in 1868 and his sons John and William continued the business. The "Prince Eddie" 1905 was the only steam vessel built at Harvey's. William died in 1893 and John in 1919. The firm carried on as a limited company until it closed in 1921. The Harvey family were active in the community. They were considerable supporters and benefactors of the Congregational Church in the High Street. They also served at times on the Local Board of Health and the Schools Board.

David Hillyard and H. Williams in 1915 had yards on the Public Hard and River Road respectively. Williams, at Britannia works, were yacht and motor launch builders and marine engineers. During the First World War they also made hulls for seaplanes which were assembled at Middleton (just west of Littlehampton). The Thompson Company assembled float planes at Middleton with a staff rising to 900 at a peak during the war. The armaments manufacture stopped dramatically at the end of the war, but Williams ship-building business survived until 1938.

David Hillyard came from Essex where he learned his trade as a builder of smaller boats. He came to Littlehampton in 1906 to work on building lifeboats. His employer's business failed after a short time but Hillyard opted to set up a small repair business in River Road. He had a great deal of business from the Admiralty during the First World War and moved into a yard next to Williams.

After the war he was able to focus on his idea of designing and building leisure craft. In 1923 he moved to part of Harvey's shipyard on the west bank. He built on average about 30 boats of varying sizes each season, including a 40-ton yacht, the largest built in Littlehampton at that time. His yachts gained a reputation for being practical and robust. Hillyard's became one of the most influential yards in the twentieth century building over 800 ships which could be found in ports all over the world. Nicholas Gray (2021) notes that of over 800 pleasure boats built in the yard, over 300 are believed still to be sailing. He says the boats were built simply, with good quality materials and largely without the use of metal components.

During the Second World War it built small craft and air sea rescue launches for the military. Hillyard's nephew Dennis Cullingford joined him in the yard after the war. Hillyard died in Littlehampton in 1963 but Cullingford carried the business on. They continued building ships until 1990 but after that turned to boat repair.

William Osborne, previously a firm of coachbuilders from London, set up in River Road as a builder and designer of motor yachts after the First World War. The firm's first boat was a 40ft cabin-cruiser launched in 1919. About 1922 William had erected hangers from the former American airbase in Rustington. These survived until 1999 when housing replaced the old riverside workshops.

In the 1930s William Osborne moved his business to part of Harvey's yard on the west bank producing cruising yachts, 15 or more a season. When William died, he was succeeded by his son William Osborne Jnr. During the Second World War they built

Illustration 33. Osborne's works 1922
(Greaves Collection)

Fairmile motor-gunboats, landing craft, storage tenders, high-speed launches and a number of boats for the Thames River Police, plus ancillary work on the Mulberry harbour. They later also built and repaired lifeboats for the Royal National Lifeboat Institute.

Joseph Robinson was one of the largest ship owners in Littlehampton, but was not involved in ship-building. He set up his ocean-going shipping business trading as the White Horse Flag line. Most if not all of his 9 ships over 300 tonnes owned in 1880 (out of 11 registered in the port) rarely visited Littlehampton but sailed far afield around the world. He had the "Trossochs" built at Harvey's yard in 1877. One of its earliest roles was to take shepherds and sheep to the Falkland Islands.

With the eclipse of sail by steam, Robinson was later restricted to coastwise routes chiefly in the coal trade. Robinson was active in local politics, serving on the Local Board of Health and then as the first chairman of the Littlehampton Urban District Council. He died in 1917 at the age of 91.

Related businesses

John Ede Butt established a timber yard in Terminus Road in the 1820s and by 1853 employed over 60 men. Butts provided the wood for the first chain ferry built in 1824 in Thomas Isemonger's yard in River Road. In 1841 John Ede Butt was a dominant figure in the timber trade at his Terminus Road site where he had steam powered sawmills with a tall chimney and by 1847 was referred to as a merchant. He also set up a business in Brighton which was connected by his own private telephone line

In 1856 he agreed a 21-year lease of Ferry Wharf from William & Albion Ockenden for the sum of £20 per annum. Later he acquired Norfolk Wharf by the river and eventually the business had also taken over Old Quay Wharf and Baltic Wharf by the public hard where he set up a timber yard, sawmill and slate merchants in

Pier Road. The majority of the imported timber came from the Baltic, hence the name Baltic Wharf. It was partly demolished in 1940. This site was taken over by Travis Arnold (later Perkins) and finally removed in 1970 to make way for riverside apartments. John E Butt passed away in 1868.

Illustration 65. Swing Bridge in operation
(Greaves Collection)

Illustration 66. Harry Joseph's Pierrots
(Littlehampton Museum Collection)

Chapter 4

Entertainment

This too is an area where technology would radically alter how people were entertained. In the first half of the nineteenth century entertainment was necessarily live, and most households organised quite a bit of entertainment amongst themselves, playing cards, singing round the piano and so on. Littlehampton boasted an amateur band as well. There were occasional street entertainers, and especially at the end of May Littlehampton had its annual fair which attracted many entertainments and brought in an audience from several miles around. It was held on Fisherman's Hard until it re-located in 1933.

By 1930 people could go to the cinema where sound had arrived and colour would soon follow. In their homes a national radio service (the BBC) was now available. In the summer there were concert parties and variety artists for the visitors, as well as Punch and Judy.

Curiously, Littlehampton also boasted a theatre of sorts in the early part of the century. Robert Elleray (2006) writes that a barn in the High Street was in use as a theatre in Littlehampton in 1808. At the time Littlehampton had a population of about 600, which makes it astonishing that it should have a functioning theatre. However, in addition to its temporary population of sailors and others using the port, the town was swollen during the 1803-1815 period by a significant number of soldiers, and the handbill makes clear that the entertainment proposed had been commissioned by the Royal North Gloucester Regiment. Elleray also cites an 1825 handbill where a Worthing theatrical company put on a show commissioned by John Olliver in the same theatre.

The Brighton Gazette (June 1827) reports that Charles Kean gave a performance at Worthing, supported by the Littlehampton theatre company, and was supposed also to perform at Littlehampton but failed to do so. They were brought to Worthing by Mr Burton, who is again referred to on 28 September 1848 when his 'corps dramatique' were said to have performed in a 'gas-lighted and conveniently fitted-up barn' in Littlehampton.

Another type of event reported in the paper is sport. It seems that Littlehampton had an established cricket team and occasional reports appear of matches against teams along the coast, such as Lancing. Not enough detail is given to suggest how the team was organized, nor who played for it, but it is clear regular cricket matches were a feature of life in Littlehampton from the beginning of this period. Nonetheless, a regular cricket club was not established until towards the end of the century.

In the 1830s the Earl of Surrey was heavily involved in the organisation of horse races along the beach. On several occasions a reception was given after the races in Surrey House and sometimes a ball. The Morning Post of October 1836 describes the event as being 'honoured by the presence of most of the nobility' in the area. By 1854 the railway had changed all that. A report in the Sussex Advertiser notes that this is now an all-day event with a regatta in the morning and races in the afternoon. In 1854 Mr Harvey also took the opportunity to have a public launch of a new ship, the Cumbria, in between the two parts of the programme. There was a dinner in the evening at the Norfolk Hotel.

Littlehampton was bedecked in bunting and flags, including both the ships in the harbour and many houses in the town. The railway company had laid on extra trains and offered attractive excursion prices as well as lending its band. The paper said that between three and four thousand people watched the regatta and double that the races in the afternoon. It is clear from the newspapers that the railway company took an active role in supporting events such as this and the Goodwood races, with the aim of selling seats on the railway.

It is also clear that the ease of access by rail meant that what had been small, local events previously were able to expand into regional events attracting large numbers of people from up and down the coast. It also seems to encapsulate the idea that while the early events had been dominated by the aristocracy and were run with their amusement in mind, the later events were focussed on a much larger audience of middle-class people who could afford to devote a midweek day to an outing to Littlehampton.

The green behind the beach was increasingly used for entertainment. In the 1860s there are reports of travelling circuses setting up on the green for a short stay. The annual Guy Fawkes Night bonfire and fireworks were also well established.

In 1861 the Congregational church had been built at the Western end of the High Street (now called the Littlehampton United Church). The building was soon expanded to include a Lecture Hall and this became (and remains) a key venue for public events

Illustration 34. The Congregational Church and Manse 1863
(Greaves Collection)

in the town centre. Visiting speakers would give presentations there, and there were also stage acts and similar performances. The National School was also occasionally used for concerts. By the 1880s Littlehampton had both an amateur choral society and an amateur orchestra.

Sports

Occasional cricket matches were reported from the early part of the nineteenth century but it was only in the second half that there was a regular cricket club. In the 1870s Rev Philpott ran a boys' school on South Terrace. He was a keen cricketer and often to be found promoting local matches. Once the cricket club was established, the members launched a cricket week which typically took place early in August and attracted a lot of visitors. In 1896 a distinguished participant was Arthur Conan Doyle.

However, one the main focuses of activity was rowing. During the 1870s and after, regattas became a major activity along the coast with all the main resorts except Brighton promoting an annual regatta and sending teams to compete in other regattas. There was an organising committee of rowing clubs which met to fix the dates and rules of these competitions. The Littlehampton club seems to have been very successful, to the point that the organisers tried to change the definition of amateur to exclude not only people who earned their living from boating, but also people who built boats or had any boat-related activity. This was perceived by Littlehampton as an attempt to disqualify a large part of its rowers.

Football took hold in the 1880s and from then on there was a significant following with matches played against teams from Arundel, Bognor, Worthing and the like. Tennis started to appear in the newspapers in the 1880s. There were regular tournaments with neighbouring towns. The town also boasted an annual sports day which also took place in August and also entertained the tourists.

By 1889 the town also boasted a golf course (albeit technically in the parish of Clymping). The army seems to have stopped using its rifle range on the west bank of the Arun in 1888. The Littlehampton men (women were not initially allowed to play), supported not least by Archie Constable the brewer, were keen to take over the land and convert it to a golf course. According to Wiseman (2016) the land was rented from four different owners and initially they only built nine holes. A clubhouse was built in 1894 and by 1921 the land had been consolidated into a single entity with eighteen holes. Members held regular tournaments.

In 1891 a cycling club was formed. It organised regular group excursions from Littlehampton with The Lamb at Angmering and The Black Rabbit at Arundel being favourite stopping places. Littlehampton also had a flourishing garden society which held monthly exhibitions during the summer months.

After the turn of the century a Motor Boat Club was formed and enjoyed great success. The club organised a series of events across the summer, including hosting a national competition.

Illustration 35. Pleasure boat on the River Arun 1922
(Greaves Collection)

The First World War brought an abrupt end to many of the sporting activities. When war was declared at the beginning of August 1914 the cricket club curtailed its programme and then in effect closed down for the duration of the war. It started up again in 1919. The football club's 1914/15 season was simply abandoned and many members joined up – and several of them lost their lives in the war.

Indoor social activities

The very active outdoor social life was accompanied by an equally active indoor life. The town had a choral society which regularly gave concerts, usually in the Lecture Hall, using soloists hired in for the occasion. The musical side also included an amateur brass band and a drum and pipe band which were much in demand across the area to enliven social events.

There was a thriving chess club, led for a while by a Professor André. He appears to have been an impresario who ran a series of Swiss choirs performing around the world. He came to live in Littlehampton and eventually died there. The chess club too engaged in competitions with neighbouring towns. On one memorable occasion a competition was organised with Worthing using a private telephone line to transmit moves. The line belonged to the Littlehampton firm of John Ede Butt which had a yard in Worthing and had had the phone installed.

By 1890 there was a Mutual Improvement Society and branches of national friendly societies such as the Ancient Order of Foresters. A reading room was opened in Surrey Street. It seems from the newspapers that its equipment included at least one billiards table, and some members objected strongly to betting going on there.

As with the outdoor activities, the First World War imposed an abrupt change on social life. Many people volunteered but there were also many urgent activities for those staying at home, including the Volunteer Training Corps, collecting money to support the temporary Red Cross Hospital in Fitzalan Road and other activities connected to the war. However, considerable though the effort was, all was wound down quickly at the end of the war and 1919 saw the resumption of the previous social life.

Concert halls and theatres

We have found no reference to Elleray's barn-theatre in the High Street after 1848, other than in Ayles, Gray and Redman (1996) who reproduce a photograph of the old barn advertising 'animated pictures'. They note that the barn was demolished in 1897. Once the Congregational Church built its Lecture Hall in 1865, this became the most regularly cited venue for all sorts of events, ranging from public lectures and political hustings through to concerts and fund-raising events for various local causes. The other popular venue in the 1870s was the National Schools in East Street, which were also used for meetings of the Local Board of Health and of course the Schools Board. St Mary's had a church hall which was demolished in 1871.

A break-away Episcopalian Reform church dedicated to St Saviour was built in New Road in 1878. The church shortly after built an adjoining church hall. St. Saviour's was of course outside the Church of England structure (and indeed the Bishop of Chichester delivered dire warnings about anyone worshipping there when it was opened) and depended on voluntary contributions. The incumbent fell ill (he died in August 1890) so an assistant was appointed. However, disagreements arose and the congregation broke up. The church was sold in June 1890 and started to be used as a concert venue, called the Victoria Hall. Confusingly the church hall next door was re-named St Mary's Hall and was also used for public events.

The Victoria Hall was the subject of great controversy in 1893 when 'Professor' Pelham applied to the Arundel magistrates for a theatrical licence for the two halls. Pelham was a well-known Littlehampton character who was an accomplished entertainer as a ventriloquist and a magician, as well as an experienced pleasure boat operator and coxswain of the Littlehampton lifeboat.

Charles Pelham appears In Kelly's Directory as living in Pier Road. Assuming there was only one Charles Pelham in Littlehampton, he also had a licence to rent bathing machines on the beach. He seems to have been a willing entrepreneur in serving Littlehampton's resort trade with boat trips for visitors, bathing and theatrical entertainments.

He often appeared as a performer in local fund-raiser entertainments and now seemed to want to become a theatre manager and impresario. He proposed making the Victoria Hall a theatre; this included opening up a new stage entrance to the hall and connecting it to St Mary's Hall, which would be used as dressing rooms for the performers.

When the matter was put to the bench, there was strong opposition from William Harvey, the shipbuilder and member of the Local Board, who argued that the local residents had built their houses close to a church and did not want the church to

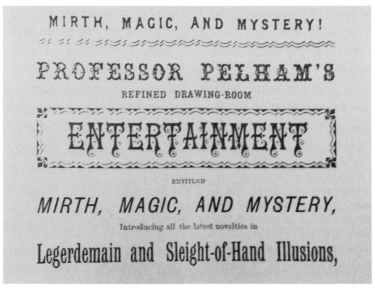

Illustration 36. Handbill advertising Professor Pelham

become a centre for noise and nuisance. He referred to the building always as St Saviour's, rather than the Victoria Hall. He did not think it appropriate to convert a consecrated building into a place of entertainment. He did not object to Littlehampton having a theatre, but it should not be in a residential street.

In a subsequent interview with the *West Sussex County Times* (25th March 1893) it also became clear that when St Saviour's was built, Harvey's sister had paid for a stained-glass window to be installed in the church, and was upset at this being incorporated into a theatre.

The magistrates refused to make a decision without hearing from the Littlehampton Local Board. The Board duly considered the question at its next meeting, but chairman John Whitehead in turn refused to debate it. He ruled that the Board was not empowered to grant theatrical licences and could not give an opinion. It noted only that its surveyor had reviewed the proposed alterations and had no objections on planning grounds.

The Littlehampton Ratepayers' Association[6] held a noisy meeting at which it expressed its support for the proposed theatre, while W B Harvey canvassed more support from residents in the area. The application came back to the magistrates and this time the licence was awarded. At the hearing Mr Harvey again voiced his objections to a theatre replacing a church and noted that it should not be on consecrated ground. One of the magistrates countered that the land had been leased and that precluded consecration.

Another resident, Mr Sida, reported that he had been to Worthing and Bognor and seen that no houses were built anywhere near the theatres in those towns. The chairman of the magistrates suggested it would be better that the building had a theatrical licence because then it would be subject to strict controls on its opening whereas currently it could stay open all hours.

---

[6] This organisation disappeared before the First World War. However a new body, the Local Government Electors Association, was formed in the 1920s and subsequently changed its name to the Ratepayers' Association.

The license was granted by the magistrates subject to it applying to the Victoria Hall and St Mary's Hall together and various alterations being made to improve access. They also specified that Mr Harvey should be allowed to remove the stained-glass window and replace it with a plain one.

The *West Sussex County Times* welcomed this as Littlehampton's first theatre, noting that there was otherwise nothing for visitors to do if the weather was poor. It suggested that without entertainment visitors would be inclined to move to the adjacent resorts with artificial facilities in addition to the natural ones.

However, even if the Victoria Hall had a theatrical license, it would be somewhat generous to call it a proper theatre. To the enthusiast a theatre would normally have a raked auditorium (the floor sloping upwards towards the back of the auditorium to improve sight lines) and a raked stage (the stage sloping up towards the back wall for the same reason); it would have at least a circle (also raked) and the stage would have a fly tower (the scenery could be held on ropes above the stage and be lowered in as required). As far as we know, Littlehampton has sadly never had such a theatre. The Victoria Hall would have had a flat floor and a raised flat stage, and would have been called a pavilion or assembly room in some resorts.

The question of a theatre for the town was a vexed one throughout this period. On the one hand, many people thought it was a necessary facility for a respectable sea-side resort. On the other, it was doubtful if anyone could make it pay consistently. Other than by Charles Pelham, the nettle seems never to have been grasped. In the event, Mr Pelham's venture does not seem to have lasted for long. The former church building was sold to the local Methodist congregation in 1896.

One of the difficulties of analysing Littlehampton's entertainment capacity is the fact that buildings frequently changed names over their lives, even if their use did not necessarily change. The hall attached to St Saviour's was known as St Mary's Hall for a while, even if it was not attached to St Mary's church, and when there had earlier been a similarly named hall that was part of that church.

In this connection there are numerous mentions of the Jubilee Hall, also in New Road. Some people suggest that this was the same building as either St Mary's Hall or the Victoria Hall. However, the Victoria County History says (p164) that 'Assembly Rooms in New Road, later called the Victoria Hall, were erected to commemorate Queen Victoria's Jubilee in 1887'.

Illustration 37. Terminus Hotel
(Greaves Collection)

The Terminus Hotel also had a concert hall which appears occasionally in the newspapers as having 'smoking concerts' (the Terminus Hotel was presumably also able to sell alcoholic drinks, which the other venues could not). Kelly's Directory for 1911 describes this as being used for theatrical entertainments and banquets and being capable of seating 500 people. The Victoria County History describes the Terminus Hall as occupying a site opposite the railway station (also the site of the Terminus Hotel) and being able to seat about 500 people. It says it created a roller-skating rink in 1909 which in turn later became a cinema.

Elleray (2006) does not mention the Terminus Hall in his gazetteer of Littlehampton theatres, but it is clear from the newspapers that as the town grew in size and in popularity as a resort between 1890 and 1914, the Terminus Hall was promoted more and more as a theatre. In particular a lessee called Wally Rice seems to have been particularly active before the First World War in promoting all sorts of entertainments, including plays and cinematic representations

First boom period

The twenty-five years before the start of the First World War were a boom period for Littlehampton as a middle-class resort, even if the town had yet to start thinking of itself as a resort, rather than a dwindling port. Pelham's conversion of St Saviour's is indicative of the visitor population reaching a size where there was a market for such entertainments. He staged two shows a week (i.e. playing for three days each), usually with visiting artists or companies.

However, there was a geographical split in the provision of entertainment between the beach area and the town centre. In many resorts the seaside entertainment is to be found on the promenade, just off the beach. But in Littlehampton this area was set aside for the green, and beyond that were only houses and hotels. Arguably there were two entertainments streams: one on the green, performing during the day and aimed at families on the beach, and the other in the town, providing evening entertainment.

Once the Littlehampton Urban District Council (LUDC) leased the green and foreshore from the Duchy of Norfolk (1898), it set up its Green and Foreshore Committee to control entertainment and commercial activity in that area. For the most part it offered concessions to independent operators who paid a rent for a licence to trade at that time. The council also built a bandstand at the eastern end of the green, where the Victoria County History says that bands played from 1903. The Duke of Norfolk provided a new bandstand in 1913 in Banjo Road.

The LUDC either rented a concession to a band (for example the Blue Hungarian Band paid 1/- per night to play on Sunday evenings) or itself engaged bands to play during the summer, with collections taken from people listening in nearby deckchairs. The Duke of Norfolk for a number of seasons offered the services of the band of the fourth battalion of the Royal Sussex Regiment, provided at his expense.

At the beach regular performers like Harry Joseph and his concert party (from 1892) and Dan Randall and then later Fred Spencer (from 1914) would erect a pop-up stage on the green, with people watching from deck-chairs and paying in to a collection, as compared to the Victoria Hall where people bought tickets and had formal seats in the normal way. Carolyn Brown (1991) says that Harry Joseph also appeared at the Victoria Hall. The council in the early years licensed two 'pitches' on the green, of which one was regularly taken by Harry Joseph for his 'pagoda' stage. Dan Randall was often the concessionaire of the second. They paid £60 a season each.

Illustration 38. Fred Spencer
(Littlehampton Museum Collection)

From 1910 there was a fairly rapid expansion of the entertainment provision, with moves to build indoor facilities and the arrival of film. The Council became more proactive and also attempted to keep more revenue for itself. At first, there was some concern

Illustration 39. Bandstand and Shelter Hall c1915
(Greaves Collection)

that there was nowhere for people to go if the weather was unpleasant, so in 1910 the council built a public shelter on the green, not far from the oyster pond.

The shelter, known at this time as the Shelter Hall, had a stage. While people had free access during the day, the Council provided that the shelter could be used for an entertainment after 6pm. In 1910 the Council also asked for competitive tenders for the two concessions to stage shows in the green. Dan Randall won pitch no 1 with a bid of £130 (Harry Joseph bid £120). Pitch No 1 carried with it the right to use the public shelter in the evening. Harry Joseph had to be content with Pitch No 2, for which he paid £100.

The pitches had become more sophisticated, with Harry Joseph erecting an awning over his to protect the audience. This however attracted the ire of the residents in South Terrace. They held their properties on long leases from the Duchy of Norfolk, which in turn guaranteed that the green in front of the buildings would be kept free of disturbance. Lt Col Mostyn, the estate manager, was called in and established that they were not concerned about the actual shows, but only the awning.

The issue rumbled on, with suggestions that the holder of the no 2, easterly pitch could use the local shelter in the evenings. However, by 1913 the no 2 pitch had disappeared and only the no 1 pitch was available, and won by Harry Joseph, who also operated the Kursaal for the first time that year. A rather sad unintended consequence was an appeal from a Derby cinema manager for funds to help pay for Dan Randall's stay in a mental hospital. The appeal cited Randall's sixteen years working in Littlehampton and said his failure to win a pitch had caused a breakdown.

It seems that Harry Joseph was not too happy with the arrangements because he opened a new theatre, the Kursaal in 1913. The Kursaal was in the area between the oyster pond and the old battery and could show films as well as stage shows. However, Harry Joseph was to be found complaining at the end of 1913 that his show on the no 1 pitch had not done well and asking for his agreed rent of £160 to be reduced to £80. He complained that his pitch had been disturbed by works relating to the drainage system during the summer, but the town councillors noted that he was competing with himself at the Kursaal.

Eventually (June 1914), the LUDC took Joseph to court for the balance of his 1913 fee. Joseph argued that his business had suffered greatly because of works going on near the site in connection with the sewage system. He asserted that his audience had to walk through mud, and the performances were often drowned out by the movement of heavy machinery. The council rejected his plea, arguing that he had tendered £160 for the site, without pre-conditions. The court found for the LUDC, and that does appear to be the last time Joseph did any theatrical business with the Council (although in the 1920s he rented a kiosk by the beach to sell a game he had invented).

Harry Joseph seems to have operated as a show business entrepreneur, based on Littlehampton. He told the court that he had provided concerts on the sea front for the last 12 years and was a popular character in the locality as a performer. The season

Illustration 40. Harry Joseph's Pierrots
(Littlehampton Museum Collection)

at Littlehampton usually lasted about 16 weeks and during the rest of the year it was pantomimes, tours or no work. He also appeared often in Worthing. Later he seems to have produced pantomimes and other entertainments for other promoters in different parts of the country. He must have had a production office in Littlehampton, and can be found advertising for staff in the local papers. He was the nearest thing the town had to its own impresario.

Developments in town

The boom in entertainment was also manifest in the rapid construction of what was originally described as a skating rink on Church Street, near St Mary's church. This was first called the Olympic Hall, and featured a maple floor for roller-skating and an extension outside with a partition that could be opened to permit skaters to continue to the outside if they wanted to. The operation was financed by what the newspapers called a 'local syndicate', chaired by Mr Frank Nye, a Littlehampton councillor and businessman, and run by a professional manager brought down from London.

At the opening, in March 1910, the chairman of the council welcomed the new building, commenting that the town needed an indoor entertainment facility, and especially one so much bigger than the others, which would permit larger gatherings. Mr Nye agreed that while the exterior was not 'a thing of beauty', it had been designed with a view to permitting the staging of theatrical events as well, and on a scale that other venues could not provide. When it was operating as a cinema after the war, its capacity was given as 760 seats.

The management organised a series of events such as fancy-dress balls and carnivals on skates to attract custom. Such was the interest created that even the Duchess of Norfolk spent an afternoon there. Nonetheless, the hall was provided with a temporary stage and could host concerts and theatrical entertainments. By the summer of 1911 the Olympic was featuring visiting theatrical entertainments that performed just for one or two nights and moved on.

The Terminus Hall was used solely as a cinema that season, and was now run by a film enthusiast, a Desmond Holderness, in partnership with a local man, Charles Shepherd. His film programme changed twice a week. However, he was a film maker as well as exhibitor and his programme often featured short films of local events. He shot these and they were on the screen in two or three days. By 1912 the Olympic Hall was also showing films regularly out of season as well as operating in season as a theatre, and all year round as a skating rink. Such was the enthusiasm for skating that a 'rink hockey' club was formed which competed with similar groups from Worthing, Chichester and Bognor.

However, in 1913 Frank Nye sold up and left Littlehampton. No explanation is given in the newspapers, but he is reported to have spent fifteen years in Littlehampton where he traded successfully, eventually opening several branches of his shop. The 1911 Kelly's directory shows him as operating dairies in New Road, Beach Road and Cornwall Road. He served as a member of the council for three years and was the first chairman of the Littlehampton Traders' Association. He was the originator of the Olympic Hall syndicate and had a number of side interests including the football club and the Philharmonic Society. He was a supporter of the Congregational church.

Late in 1913, several months after his departure, the Olympic Hall was acquired by Mr Shepherd and Mr Holderness, of the Electric Picture Palace. They re-named the building the Empire Cinema and installed the latest projection equipment. There were some concerns that skating would have to stop, but a policy of mixed use was continued, with the building available for skating three times a week, and presenting films and live theatre as well.

Illustration 41 Olympic Hall later Empire then Palladium Cinema (Greaves Collection))

Cinemas

Films started to be shown in the UK towards the end of the nineteenth century, but it took several decades before the industry settled into its formula (which disappeared again in the 1970s) of a programme consisting of two 90-minute features shown in an ornate, purpose-built cinema. In the early years commercial films were short, and were often shown in theatres. Variety theatres especially were happy to install equipment and show a ten-minute film in the middle of a programme of variety acts. At some resorts enterprising managers would erect marquees and show films on the beach. For several years films were shown regularly by touring cinema shows in special halls and also in buildings with other uses, as was probably the case at the old barn theatre.

However, projecting those early films was technically challenging. The projector would only take a reel lasting ten minutes, so normally you would need to install two projectors with the ability to switch between them every ten minutes. The life of a projectionist was not one of leisure watching films, but rather running from one projector to another to take off the old reel, re-wind it ready for the next performance and fit the new reel - while keeping them all in the right order.

The film carried cue marks in the top right-hand corner of the screen. These gave first a ten-second warning, at which the projectionist should start the leader running on the second projector, and then at the second cue, open up the blind in front of the second projector and close the first. On screen the picture would shift either to a new scene, or a different camera angle on a continuing scene, so that the change of projectors was not apparent to the audience.

The other major problem was the intensity of the light source. The light had to project a large image through several hundred feet, and an electric filament could not produce the required intensity. The projectors, up to and including the 1970s, used carbon arc lights. These produced an intense light by passing a very high voltage current across two carbon terminals. The carbon rods used to make the light burned down systematically and another vital part of the projectionist's job was to advance them together as they were consumed, This required constant attention, interspersed with occasional panics if a rod had been damaged before installation and a piece dropped off in mid-reel.

The actual material used for the film itself was highly flammable and was capable of spontaneous combustion. The carbon-arc light developed a very high temperature and therefore, if the film became stuck in the gate where light was passed through it, it could easily burn. Fire was a significant hazard, and potentially life-threatening, given the number of people present in a confined space.

In effect, anyone wishing to start showing films needed a substantial investment in equipment plus a high-power electricity source well beyond what was used domestically, as well as trained staff to run the projection.

The Terminus Hall started to show occasional films in 1909, alongside a major live theatre activity. However, these were so popular that by 1911 it had been reconfigured as the Electric Picture Palace. It was unusual in having a screen made of plaster, and its own generator to develop a powerful enough current to operate the carbon-arc lamps. However, disaster struck in August 1914 when a fire in one of the projectors soon spread to the rest of the theatre, despite the best attentions of the fire brigade. Since Shepherd and Holderness now controlled the Empire as well, they simply concentrated their programme there. It may have been a relief to them in that the outbreak of war had seriously upset the distribution of films.

According to Eyles, Gray and Readman (1996) the cinema was nonetheless swiftly restored and re-opened in September 1914, with added safety features to protect the auditorium from any possible fire in the 'lantern room'. However, Eyles, Grey and Readman (1996) point out that in 1915 the licence was in the name of Maurice Mansbridge, reverting to Shepherd in 1924. In 1930 the Shepherd family sold the Electric Picture Palace to an established cinema partnership (Filer and Shinebaum). The following year it was refurbished, a sound system was installed and it re-opened in March 1931 as the Regent. It was the smallest of the Littlehampton cinemas, with only 650 seats, and was the first to stop operating as a cinema, in 1960. It was used for bingo for a while but the building was used for storage after 1974.

The Palladium

Roller-skating was a popular pastime in 1910 when the Olympic Hall was built but the building was capable of being used as a theatre. When it was taken over by Charles Shepherd and Desmond Holderness in 1913, it continued to operate as a multifunctional building with some roller-skating, films, live theatre and occasional concerts. Desmond Holderness disappeared from the management in about 1914, probably to join up. In 1916 it was taken over by Harry Joseph, who changed its name to the Palladium. Joseph continued through the war but appears to have given up in 1920.

The cinema continued to be owned by the Shepherd family until they sold out in 1930 to the Filer and Shinebaum partnership who immediately installed a sound system. Littlehampton had its first 'talkies'. It closed in 1986 – its presence is reflected only in the name of the *Amenic Court* block of flats on the site today.

In fact, when Harry Joseph gave up the Palladium, he filed for bankruptcy and in the court hearings (February 1922) he cited the Palladium as the source of his troubles. He told the court that when he acquired the premises 'it was quite devoid of fittings or furniture, even the handles of the doors had been removed.' He added that he had lost money on the place in 1916, 1917 and 1918; he said he had lost about £800 overall. Mr Joseph was resident in Littlehampton, his wife owned the

Illustration 42. Harry Joseph (Littlehampton Museum Collection)

Kursaal, and after the bankruptcy he continued to work in the entertainment sector until his death in 1932.

During the war the town remained quite busy as a resort, and its entertainment offering continued. The outbreak of war caused people in August 1914 to cancel and stay at home, but even by September the holiday business was back (at that time the season ran to the beginning of October). The Council noted a drop of about 20%-25% in bridge tolls which would be consistent with a fall in traffic. However, in 1915 the town was reporting that all accommodation was pretty well full. The major difference was that the railway company was no longer operating any excursion trains, so there was a major drop in day visitors.

Entertainment was hit in a number of ways – the Blue Hungarian Band for example returned to Austria in August 1914, and other bands and pierrot troupes lost young performers who volunteered for the services. Nonetheless Fred Spencer arrived on the scene and mounted his concert party on the green, while Harry Joseph was at the Kursaal (which he re-named the Casino, supposedly because of a desire to distance himself from a German-sounding name).

The Council, though, took the view that they should not be providing bands during the war. Although this was contested by those who said that the town should do its best to entertain so that people would come back after the war. The popular view was that many people took holidays on the South coast during the war who would normally have gone elsewhere. It was 1917 before the Council engaged a band – and then for only six weeks.

After the war – a professional resort

As is apparent, the First World War brought to an end the informal expansion of the resort and the services intended to entertain the visitor. There was the inevitable shortage of manpower, significant inflation (an accumulated 100% from 1914 to 1919), and an absence of excursionists. The Council reined in expenditure as well. After the war the economy was slow to pick up again, and the theatre offer changed further.

The years between the wars were difficult with the economy going through significant periods of depression. Nevertheless, for Littlehampton it was from this time that the Council really thought of the town as a resort and made significant attempts to expand and improve. It was helped in this by the formation of a Chamber of Commerce which did much to influence the advertising of the resort and point out where the Council could improve.

The Council's specialist committee was now re-named the Pleasure Grounds and Foreshore Committee to take in the idea that its remit now included tennis courts and a bowling green which the Council had built on land given by the Duke of Norfolk between Maltravers Drive and St Winifride's Road. The 15th Duke had provided the land before the war, but development had been halted when the war broke out.

The committee appointed a full-time entertainments manager to coordinate the various money-making schemes run by the

Illustration 43. Blue Hungarian Band
(Littlehampton Museum Collection)

Council. Progressively the Council was moving away from the model of renting concessions to third parties, to directly managing services itself. Before the war it had taken the renting of deckchairs in-house and started to rent out individual bathing huts instead of leaving intermediaries to do this.

Based on feedback from people listening to visiting military bands, the Council decided to erect shelters around the new bandstand in Banjo Road. Because the Council's lease was an annual one, there was some legal difficulties in doing this, the shelters were not complete until 1922.

There was a very significant change in policy towards the concert-parties. Instead of renting sites to independent producers for the whole season, the Council became a theatrical manager. Charles Doré, the entertainments manager, persuaded the Council to join a south coast syndicate and present a series of different entertainments during the summer in the Shelter Hall (which was beginning to be styled the Pavilion on the Green) instead of renting to one producer. The idea was that the syndicate booked productions, which were rotated round the syndicate's theatres. This worked spectacularly well, and the Pleasure Grounds and Foreshore Committee was able to report a significant increase in revenues and a profit of more than £350 on the 1923 season.

Mr Doré then persuaded the Council to install heating in the Pavilion so that it could be used in the winter. Once that was available, he produced a number of amateur dramatic shows out of season and there were visiting productions on special occasions. In the 1924 he repeated the syndicate presentations with the same success. A headliner in 1924 was a young Arthur Askey.

Harry Joseph continued to be visible on the entertainment scene. In the 1920s his daughter, whose stage name was Lena Jay, had a licence for what was styled the Norfolk Quay Pavilion, where she ran Pierrot shows (featuring her father, of course). There are several mentions of this 'pavilion' in the Littlehampton Gazette, but that is the only reference we could find. Norfolk Quay is on the East bank of the river in a stretch where River Road has turned in to Surrey Street and Pier Road has not yet reached the river. This is more or less where the lifeboat station is to be found today.

Another innovation was the opening of 'The Bungalow', a set of tea-rooms in Beach Road. Although billed as tea-rooms, in fact the Bungalow offered tea dances and a regular weekly evening dance between the wars, as well as occasional whist drives and other functions. The success of the dances must have alerted others to the opportunities. The Beach Hotel started to run a weekly dance as well. Despite being a popular venue, its owner declared bankruptcy at the end of 1927. William Bigg said he had bought it in May 1925 and had had a good season, but both 1926 and 1927 had been poor and he had fallen behind with the rent and his loan repayments. The business was taken over by the company running the Beach Hotel.

Mr Doré, the Council's entertainments manager, proposed after the 1925 season that a small area of the band enclosure should be surfaced to dancing. This was done and helped the Council

Illustration 44. The Bungalow
(Littlehampton Museum Collection)

to decide to make the enclosure more elaborate and add a tea room as well as a band room and an office for Mr Doré. Not everyone was happy about the dancing, but the Council went ahead anyway.

However, it ran into trouble with the Duchy Estate Office who would not give permission for it to be built. After negotiation it was agreed that the more elaborate enclosure with a roof could be built in time for the 1927 season, but refreshments could not be sold. After the building had started to operate, the Estate Office relented on the issue of refreshments. The Council experimented with weekly dances over the Christmas period as well.

The 1928 season started well with the new dancing facilities. What had up until then been styled the 'band enclosure' started to be referred to as the 'Dance Pavilion', while the Shelter Hall was now definitely the 'Pavilion on the Green'. However, one Sunday night at the beginning of July a fire broke out and the new Dance Pavilion was largely destroyed.

Astonishingly it was re-built in two weeks and back in business for the bulk of the season. Linfield's, a large local firm of builders, rose to the challenge and worked night and day to recreate a viable shelter and dance floor. Fortunately, the bandstand as such was not touched, the damage was primarily to the southern end of the enclosure. Band performances continued and dances re-started after two weeks.

Mr Doré's arrangements were working well and by 1930 the Council was budgeting an annual contribution of £2,000 from the Pleasure Grounds and Foreshore Committee. It also had about £3,000 a year from net bridge tolls as well as a growing revenue from car parking. Unfortunately, 1930 and 1931 were very poor seasons for the resort and the resort activities run by the Council were showing losses.

Mr Doré made the unfortunate decision in the autumn of 1931 to ask for a four-month sabbatical. This fed directly into the prejudices of certain councillors (especially Mr Phipps, a local boat operator) who had always believed that the Council did not need an entertainments manager and should just rent out its properties to commercial operators. He also believed that there was no work for the manager in the winter, and took the sabbatical proposal as evidence of that.

The majority of the Council defended the entertainments manager, pointing out that all the planning and contracting was done in the winter and also that in the season Mr Doré worked twelve hours a day, seven days a week. Nonetheless a petition, signed by nearly a thousand people, asking for his dismissal was presented to the Council. The Council faced down the protests, but significant economies were made in the 1932 season.

Finally in August 1933 the Council decided that Doré's post (restyled in 1932 as Foreshore, Publicity and Entertainments Manager) should only run for eight months each year. The supporters of a full-time post had had their case damaged by Doré's sabbatical. Doré accepted the decision, but then

Illustration 45. Bandstand and Dance Pavilion c1929
(Greaves Collection)

resigned in March 1934, just as he was about to re-start, to take a job at Clacton[7]. Thereafter the Council operated without an entertainments manager.

The Council faced the dilemma that it wanted the season to be as long as possible, and aimed to run band concerts, dances and shows from the Whitsun bank holiday until the end of September. However, there were not sufficient holidaymakers in June to make the entertainment profitable, and the season tailed off in September. The season's profits from the green were earned in July and August.

The Council had the choice of running unprofitable ventures at each end of the season but having something to encourage holidaymakers, as against reducing the entertainment to the most profitable periods and making the season in effect shorter. For 1932 they followed the latter course – the entertainment started in July and ended in mid-September, making a high season of about eleven weeks, against an aspirational sixteen or eighteen weeks. The Council had a choice between promoting the well-being of the town, or trying to make a profit on entertainment.

Bandstand Pavilion

In the middle of 1932 Billy Butlin's amusement park arrived. Its operations were temporary in 1932 because of the need to run as much as possible during the peak of the summer season. Its first full season was 1933, and it had sophisticated mechanical attractions and also 50 live monkeys on display. It was very popular and attracted many people, but it was also noisy, motivating the Pleasure Grounds and Foreshore Committee to decide that the Pavilion on the Green could no longer run an evening entertainment. The Pavilion reverted to its original function of providing a shelter during bad weather and the concert party activity was moved to the Dance Pavilion.

[7] Doré had been active in promoting amateur drama and opera in Littlehampton. He was invited back in 1935 to reprise the role of KoKo in The Mikado. No doubt he would have had his own little list.

The bandstand at Banjo Road had gone through several upgrades over its life, going from having shelter built around to protect from the weather those listening, to installing a dance floor, then a tea room and dressing rooms, and finally a decent stage. Its name changed from Bandstand to Dance pavilion to Bandstand Pavilion.

From this time on, members of the Council and also the Ratepayers' Association started to agitate for the building of a proper concert hall. However, many people wanted it to be in town, saying that on the green it would block the view and only be used half the year. The Council drew up plans for a hall seating 800 people with a raked auditorium and a balcony, to be built in Banjo Road which would be reconstructed to go round both sides of the hall. Eventually a dance hall would be built also. People also thought it would be loss-making and would be better done by a commercial organisation.

The subject came up repeatedly at Council meetings where it was agreed at one and rescinded at the next to be deferred and deferred. It suffered the same fate as nationalised industries in having to compete for investment with social priorities, assessed on completely different criteria. The Council was faced with having a finite limit on how much it could invest, and at this critical phase they chose municipal development with Mewsbrook Park and drainage, rather than a proper theatre.

The owners of the Palladium and the Regent cinemas applied for planning permission to build a 1,250-seat cinema in Maltravers Road near the library. This never saw the light of day either, as the Odeon chain then applied in 1935 to build an Odeon in the High Street. This was opened with great fanfare in May 1936, undoubtedly to the dismay of the other two cinemas, not only because of having to share their audience, but also because the Odeon would always get priority from film distributors in booking the best films.

According to Eyles, Gray and Readman (1996) the new building had an imposing foyer while the 'auditorium was plain but pleasant, relying primarily on concealed lighting of the ceiling to illuminate the auditorium during the intervals'. They add that as it had the advantage of strong circuit releases, the cinema did well enough in the holiday season but had to struggle during the rest of the year. They note that at about 10,000 the town population in the 1930s was very low to support three cinemas.

The later demise of the Regent would have helped the Odeon, but it remained a relatively marginal venue and was part of package sold by the Rank Organisation to Classic cinemas in 1967. The cinema was renamed the Classic, but the new owners introduced bingo on some nights of the week. They sold the cinema in 1974 to a local operator who abandoned film altogether, and the building was finally demolished in 1984.

Chapter 5

Hospitality

Another of the particular features of Littlehampton is that it has always been provided with a large number of public houses and hotel accommodation. The former can most easily be attributed to the fact that it was a booming sea port in the nineteenth century as well as having a military garrison, and the latter also to its attractions as a genteel place to take the sea air.

Pigot's directory of 1832 lists seven hostelries:

- Beach House Hotel
- Dolphin Hotel
- The George
- King's Arms
- Norfolk Hotel
- Ship and Anchor
- White Hart

According to Gwen Lansdell (1994), the King's Arms was in River Road and the Ship and Anchor in Ferry Road, with the White Hart at the bottom of Surrey Street, all within very close proximity to the river and harbour activities. The Norfolk Hotel, the Dolphin and the George were scarcely further away, running up Surrey Street to the High Street, and arguably making a link between the harbour nucleus and the growing town centre[8]. The Norfolk Hotel and the Dolphin were more upmarket and offered accommodation and stabling as well as food and drink. Famously, a young Byron spent a few summer weeks at the Dolphin in 1806.

---

[8] There is a useful map on p50 of Barrett & Greenwood's (2020) *The George Inn Littlehampton, the true story,* which also includes material on the Norfolk Hotel.

All of these establishments were already in existence at the turn of the century, except the Norfolk Hotel which opened in 1824 according to Barrett & Greenwood (2020).

The most upmarket hotel was the Beach Hotel, built in 1775 apparently in the middle of nowhere: by the beach but not immediately adjacent to either Manor Farm (which became the town centre) or Beach Town, and with no link to the river. There was only a bridle path linking it to the town until 1829 when the Earl of Surrey contributed to the construction of a carriageway (now Beach Road). The collection of houses adjacent to Surrey House in Beach Town gradually extended westwards until the new South Terrace reached the Beach Hotel.

When Peregrine Phillips stayed at the Beach Coffee House in 1778 he was impressed with the generous dimensions of the place as also its wine and food (but less its ale). Its name seems to have changed over time to Beach House Hotel (Pigot 1832) and then simply Beach Hotel (Kelly 1851).

Illustration 46. Beach Coffee House
(Littlehampton Museum Collection)

None of the trade directories of that time give any clue as to the existence of other accommodation. It is in Kelly's directory of 1859 that we find the extra label 'lodging house'. Nonetheless, it is quite clear from the newspaper reports that there was a significant lodging industry before then. For example, the *Sussex Advertiser* on 6th August 1832 reports: 'That delightful watering place, Littlehampton, is now fast filling, it having received an influx of visitors in the last few days, and many more families are expected to take up their residence there'. Probably much of the accommodation at first was houses to let and apartments, rather than boarding houses.

The *Morning Post* of 22nd September 1834 comments: 'The watering places on the Sussex coast Worthing, Hastings, Littlehampton, St Leonards and even Brighton are full to overflowing ... at Littlehampton Lady Louisa Pole, General Shrapnel, Captain and Mrs Hunter, and Commander Rich are amongst the latest arrivals.'

It seems that the 'season' ran from August to November at that time and would evidently have had more to do with the social calendar than the weather. Some Littlehampton entrepreneurs built houses in Beach Town so that they could be rented out to these seasonal visitors. Some other houses rented out sets of rooms. It is likely that the seaside accommodation industry was thriving, but was confined primarily to Beach Town in the early nineteenth century. The New Inn opened in Norfolk Road in 1833, giving Beach Town its first public house – and the only one that has lasted through to the twenty-first century.

The railway changes everything

The nature of Littlehampton's resort activity changed dramatically with the arrival of the railway in 1846. Suddenly travel became much faster and cheaper. The newspapers reported that in 1835 a stage coach took eight hours to travel from Brighton to London, while railway, which opened shortly after, did the journey in one hour fifteen minutes. The coast became easily accessible from London. Since the line from Arundel to Brighton was a feeder to the London/Brighton railway, travel along the coast was also made much easier.

The London, Brighton and South Coast Railway (LB&SCR) actively promoted tourist activity, running special excursion trains at weekends. The original Arundel and Littlehampton station (at Lyminster) was an ideal jumping off point. People would walk or take a coach the two miles down to the beach in the morning and then move up to Arundel in the afternoon. Even in the nineteenth century the Duchy of Norfolk would allow visitors into its grounds. After that the day-trippers would return to the station and on to their homes.

So popular was the day trip that the Littlehampton Local Board was moved to complain to the LB&SCR about the number of trippers they were bringing to the town on a Sunday. It cited one instance where it claimed that 7,000 people had descended on the town on a Sunday. Most businesses were closed, people were at church, and did not wish to have their Sabbath disturbed by the antics of drunken trippers from London.

Illustration 47. Nelson and Victory Hotel c1890
(Greaves Collection)

Of course, the figure of 7,000 looks to be an exaggeration, but there is no doubt that there was a tension in the town, which lasted for many years, between the traders who benefitted from the influx of visitors and the other townsfolk who did not like the disturbance. A ratepayers association was formed, somewhat in opposition to the Local Board, to challenge some of the Board's decisions and press for a more trade-friendly approach. An example would be when in 1893 Charles Pelham applied for a theatrical licence for St Saviour's – the Board refused to take a position, but the Ratepayers Association strongly supported him.

The railway facilitated not only day-trippers, but also people who stayed for a period to enjoy the sea and beach. As a consequence, there was a great expansion of the availability of accommodation, ranging from rooms to let to boarding houses and bed and breakfast establishments. It is difficult to get exact figures about this, but an analysis of Kelly's Directory gives the following information about the hospitality industry:

Year	Total Trades	Hotels/Pubs	Lodgings
1851	103	9	0
1859	143	8	13
1866	147	13	16
1878	218	16	59
1890	312	16	95
1899	566	20	207
1911	677	20	252

There is no way of knowing whether Kelly's Directory was comprehensive, nor are there any other sources of industry data at this time. However, using the Kelly's information, we can see that from 1850 there was the development of a formal hospitality industry (and also of other trades and services). The figures suggest that this made a major advance in the last decade of the nineteenth century. This is in line with the idea that before 1850 the resort aspects of Littlehampton were limited to use by a wealthy elite. After the arrival of the railway, more and more people used the resort. With the growth of a new middle class the demand for resort facilities would have increased significantly. The introduction of bank holidays would have also swelled the day-visitor trade, encouraged by the railway.

A particular aspect of the guest house industry was that it offered a rare opportunity for women, married or unmarried, to create and run a business of their own. In the nineteenth century, when a woman married, control of her fortune passed to her husband and she had no investment decision-making power. However, an unmarried woman could administer her own fortune, as could a widow, although the opportunities to operate an independent business or profession were few and far-between. The rise of the boarding house in nineteenth century resorts created a major new opportunity in this restricted area.

Illustration 48. Adverts from Town Guide 1935
(Littlehampton Museum Collection)

Of the 252 businesses offering accommodation in Littlehampton in the 1911 Kelly's Directory, 102 were listed as having women proprietors (and it is probable that many of those showing a male proprietor were actually run by women). Aside from that, women appear in 1911 mainly as dress-makers and shop-owners, and relatively few of those (perhaps ten of each). There are one or two shown as running schools or offering freelance teaching services. In Littlehampton, individual women were listed as being an artist, a bathing machine proprietor, running a registry office for servants and a refreshment room.

War intervenes

The First World War effectively put a stop to the development of the resort. Aside from the fact that many men joined up, which completely disrupted family life, there were food shortages as a result of the dangers of submarines to shipping. Eventually there was rationing but there was also considerable inflation. Over the five-year period 1914 to 1919, the cumulative inflation was one hundred percent – in effect everything cost twice as much as at the beginning of the war.

Illustration 49. The second Beach Hotel before WWI
(Littlehampton Museum Collection)

It was very difficult to run a boarding house with these supply problems, and potential clients have had less money to spend as a result of their incomes not keeping pace with inflation. Taxation also had an impact – income tax was at about 3% in the nineteenth century but reached 30% by the end of the war. With incomes being impacted by both tax and inflation, the pressure for salary increases to compensate was part of the problem of inflation. It should also be said that the threshold at which income tax became payable was high, so did not affect working people, but rather the growing middle class. However, these were the main clients of hospitality establishments at that time.

Day-tripper activity died away during the war, but surprisingly, the LB&SCR reported that passenger revenues climbed back from 1915, with enough people still keen to visit the seaside despite the war. Some resorts, such as Blackpool, actually gained business because they were selected to act as training centres. This was not the case with Littlehampton, but its accommodation was mostly full in the season despite the war.

After the war

The period between the wars was one of economic and social disruption which would have had an impact on people's ability and inclination to spend their money on leisure. In a period of economic constraint, people focus their spending on immediate necessities; discretionary spending on holidays and leisure generally is usually the first to be cut. This means that the hospitality industry is cyclical and only does really well when the economy is booming. That is mitigated to an extent by people 'trading down', for example by taking a long weekend at the beach instead of two weeks.

The inflationary effect of war was extremely disruptive to the economy. In certain sectors, such as farming and coal mining, there were wages regulatory bodies which had been reluctant to sanction wage increases to compensate for inflation. This meant that people such as coal miners were in effect earning less and less money in terms of its purchasing power. That lead finally to the General Strike of 1926, but that was the tip of the iceberg in a vast shake-out of the economy caused by inflation, and to an extent taxation.

The effect of taxation is to take money out of the commercial economy and re-direct it for government purposes. This means that demand in the 'normal' economy is restrained and businesses do not recover as quickly as they might have done. Although the great economist, John Maynard Keynes, was at this time formulating hypotheses that addressed the effect of withdrawing money from the economy, the governments between the wars did not understand how to manage the situation. When economic times were bad, they believed that you had to 'tighten the belt' (reduce expenditure) to get by, whereas Keynes eventually showed that the reverse is the case: the government needs to put money into the economy to re-float it. The government did not do that and severe economic recession was the consequence.

Despite the economic gloom, the hospitality sector was active. We have been unable to find data relating to Littlehampton. The entries in Kelly's Directory showed a dramatic decline after the first World War, but we think this is probably not so much that businesses disappeared, but rather that they realised there were better ways to advertise accommodation than in a business directory. Littlehampton UDC started to produce a Town Guide to promote the resort. It is also clear that commercial publishers were coming onto the scene and producing holiday guides.

There is an example of one of these in the Littlehampton Museum Collection: a *Homeland Pocket Book* for 1927 (see over). The Homeland guide offered information about the resort and was accompanied by adverts for boarding houses and businesses in Littlehampton – making a serious attempt to describe Littlehampton for the visitor. Not surprisingly, this model was wisely taken up by commercial publishers as a means

THE HOMELAND HANDY GUIDES

A series of inexpensive but artistically produced guides, dealing with interesting towns or small areas, beautifully illustrated and provided with plans. They deal concisely with the history and antiquities of the towns, together with their advantages as places of residence or as holiday resorts, and also contain notes on the places of interest within easy reach.

34. ASHBURTON, DEVON	..	4d.	25. NORTH WALSHAM AND THE		
33. BARNSTAPLE, DEVON..	..	6d.	NORFOLK BROADS ..	..	6d.
11. BIRCHINGTON, KENT		6d.	30. NORTHWOOD, MIDDLESEX	..	4d.
10. BRIGHTLINGSEA, ESSEX	..	6d.	16. PETWORTH, SUSSEX ..	..	6d.
8. BRIGG, LINCOLNSHIRE		4d.	20. PORTISHEAD, SOMERSET	..	6d.
36. BRIXHAM, DEVON ..	..	6d.	2. READING, BERKSHIRE	..	6d.
14. BURNHAM-ON-CROUCH, ESSEX		4d.	7. RYE AND WINCHELSEA		6d.
19. CLEVEDON, SOMERSET	..	6d.	3. SANDWICH, KENT ..	..	6d.
35. DEAL AND WALMER, KENT		6d.	6. SPALDING, LINCOLNSHIRE	..	4d.
17. GLASTONBURY, SOMERSET	..	6d.	27. TAVISTOCK, DEVON ..	..	4d.
32. HARPENDEN, HERTS ..		6d.	9. WALTON-ON-THE-NAZE, ESSEX		4d.
24. HAYLE & PHILLACK, CORNWALL		4d.	4. WATCHET, WILLITON, AND		
31. LITTLEHAMPTON, SUSSEX	..	6d.	WASHFORD, SOMERSET	..	4d.
18. MAIDSTONE, KENT ..	..	6d.	12. WESTGATE-ON-SEA, KENT	..	6d.
23. MERSEA ISLAND, ESSEX	..	6d.	28. WESTWARD HO! DEVON	..	6d.
15. MIDHURST, SUSSEX ..	..	6d.	21. WOKINGHAM, BERKSHIRE	..	4d.
13. MUNDESLEY, NORFOLK	..	6d.			

Postage 2d.

THE HOMELAND ASSOCIATION, LTD.,
37 and 38 Maiden Lane, Covent Garden, London, W.C.2.

Illustration 50. Homeland Guides to resorts
(Littlehampton Museum Collection)

of generating revenue. Advertisers would be persuaded to take an advertisement, which would then generate the revenue to publish the material – very much like free sheets today.

The West Sussex Record Office contains the 1910 and 1911 volumes of *Pike's Bognor, Littlehampton, Arundel and District Blue Book and Local Directory*, which lists boarding houses, hotels and public houses, amongst other things. It comments (p107):

> ... *the lost glory of the town* (Littlehampton) *as a sea port is, however, compensated by its ever-increasing popularity as a holiday resort ... from morn till night throughout the summer months happy, sunburnt children crowd upon the sands, while their elders find rest, quiet and health.*

Advertising

We believe that dedicated holiday guides of this kind took the place of the Kelly's Directory entries, but unfortunately there are so many guides that we have not been able to trace copies on a consistent basis of an individual guide that might provide an indicator of the growth, or decline, of the hospitality industry during this period.

Before the WWI the Council had formed a joint advertising committee made up of some councillors and business people. The 15th Duke had offered to match, pound for pound, any money put into an annual advertising pot. The Advertising Committee was given some money by the Council and then raised money by inviting donations from businesses. Their main annual advertising fell into two elements.

The railway companies ran a promotional scheme where companies in the midlands and north displayed posters from southern seaside towns in their trains. In fact, posters from this period can be collectors' items today. Littlehampton paid to be in this scheme, and it also paid to be included in a large hoarding at Olympia which advertised south coast resorts.

The Advertising Committee regularly complained that boarding house keepers and other providers of accommodation were the most niggardly in making contributions to the annual budget. However, the LUDC was also in the habit of licensing a commercial publisher each year to produce a town guide. In return for the endorsement of the Council, the printer would sell advertising to the accommodation sector and others, and then distribute free copies of the guide. Before the war, the print run was typically 2,000.

This changed after the war. In 1923 the town businessmen (and women?) got together to form a Chamber of Commerce – which can be seen as another aspect of the professionalization of the resort activity. The Chamber of Commerce was vociferous in its criticism of the advertising of the town. It joined the Advertising Committee and in 1925 persuaded the Council to take the publication of the Town Guide in house.

From 1926 onward there was therefore an official publication intended to attract holiday-makers. The Chamber of Commerce got together with the railway company to provide an information office at the station. The railway poster advertising continued but now invited people to contact Littlehampton in order to receive a copy of the Town Guide, which was also of course available at the information office.

The annual report of the Advertising Committee showed that this was effective, and boarding house owners were reputed to regard the guide as the best sales method available to them. Its print run steadily increased, reaching 10,000 in the 1930s. Unfortunately, very few copies of this guide survive. While Charles Doré, the entertainments manager, took a major role in producing it while he was in that job, his post disappeared in 1934. The Littlehampton Museum does though hold copies for a number of years from 1926, the first produced directly. The Town Guide continued after WWII but the Museum has no copies after the 1970s.

There is no doubt that the resort business was struggling a little in the 1920s and the 1930s, but according to Elleray was significantly

Illustration 51. 1926 Official Town Guide, cover (Littlehampton Museum Collection)

Illustration 52. 1926 Official Town Guide, Title page (Littlehampton Museum Collection)

revived by the 1932 opening of Billy Butlin's amusement park on the site of the old windmill, on the east bank of the river. Elleray (1991) cites a newspaper article as saying:

The amusement park ... has caused thousands of visitors to pour in by road and rail, packing the beach and foreshore to a density hitherto unknown or even dreamed of.

While people believed that Butlin's had boosted the number of day visitors, if anything, it was likely to have reduced the number of visitors spending some time in the town. It is clear from the returns of the Council's entertainment activities, that there were bad years and not so bad years, but the 1930s were not an easy time for anyone.

WWII would, of course, bring to an end this period of the resort's expansion. Both the east and west beaches were off limits because they had been mined against their possible use for a landing, and travel was heavily restricted. Up to a point the town would also be used for evacuees.

Illustration 67. Women joined the Post Office in WWI

Chapter 6

Other employment

In other sections we have reviewed different business sectors related specifically to the harbour and resort activities of Littlehampton. In this section we will also review briefly where employment was to be found outside of those specialist sectors. Farming was of course important at the start of the period, but receded over time as the fields were gradually turned over to support the town. Many were ultimately used for housing, but some were also used for public services such as the inter-denominational cemetery and the water-pumping station, to say nothing of the sports field.

Historically the land running south from the downs to the plain and then the sea were used for agriculture. In the Middle Ages they had largely been given as endowments to religious establishments that farmed them to sustain the establishment and generate income. However, the holdings were removed from their religious owners during the dissolution ofthe monasteries by Henry VIII in the late 1530s and sold off. In this process and in following years the Duchy of Norfolk was active in building up its portfolio of land and eventually became the owner of all of Littlehampton and much of the surrounding area.

Agriculture remained the dominant use until the rapid growth of Littlehampton and of popular tourism in the later part of the nineteenth century. In the early nineteenth century farmers were still breeding prize Southdown sheep and prize cattle in the area, and Littlehampton had a livestock market and an occasional corn market. An article in the Hampshire Advertiser of 1836 reports that sheep-stealing is 'a very frequent occurrence' in the neighbourhood of Littlehampton. Even as late as the First World War, the newspapers report that local farmers were being given releases from conscription and boys allowed to leave school a year earlier if it was to work on a farm. In the nineteenth century farming was still a significant area of activity in Littlehampton.

Duke and Ockenden

However, a major Littlehampton firm, Duke and Ockenden, a pioneer in sourcing freshwater supplies for drinking also established itself in Littlehampton. William Ockenden came to Littlehampton in 1802, setting up business as an ironmonger. By 1828 he was listed as both a smith and ironmonger. His business expanded and in 1838 he leased land on the river from the Duke of Norfolk; this put him in a better position to supply fittings to the local shipyards. By 1843 he had built Ferry Wharf so he could land slates which were shipped from Wales. This trade ended in 1855 when William and Albion (his youngest son) agreed a 21-year lease of the Wharf to John Ede Butt, the timber merchant.

It was in about 1850 when William moved the original blacksmith business in the High Street to River Road, and that Albion Ockenden, who possessed both enterprise and a character suited to industry superior to his brothers, became more involved in the business. In the 1845 town directory Albion is listed as a ship smith while his father was an ironmonger and smith. The Ockendens also became wheelwrights and were using a horse powered drilling machine to drill iron knees, brackets used to strengthen wooden sailing ships. They also had a punching machine which was used between 1880 and 1914 – and was later sold to Dando.

Ten years later the business moved again, into premises on the riverside which consisted of a blacksmith's shop with four forges and an engineering shop. It was here that Albion set up a business as a brass and iron founder, anchor and ship smith, ship chandler, ironmonger, brazier and the patentee of Sussex Norton tube wells.

The 1870s saw Albion Ockenden become interested in another project which ultimately led to his sons Maurice and Frederick joining R F Duke & Co, who had a timber and slate business on Old Quay Wharf. They formed the company of Duke & Ockenden, trading as Dando's Tube Well Engineers in 1887. This company bored artesian tube wells and did the initial borings and placed the caissons for the swing bridge. From then on Albion concentrated on this and passed the ironmongery business to his sons Sargent and Edmund. Dando's worked throughout the world to find water and provide deep wells.

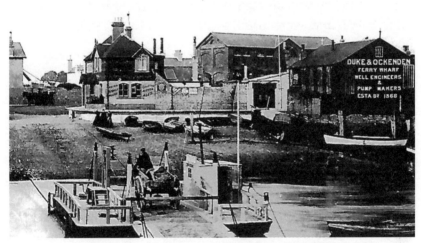

Illustration 53. Duke and Ockendon's works 1907
(Greaves Collection)

The ironmongery did continue as a separate business. When Albion's sons Sargent and Edmund took over, they opened a shop in the High Street trading as Ockenden Brothers. Although largely known as ironmongers they were diversifying into various other products but at the same time continuing to run the foundry forges. In 1899 the family company got into difficulties and was run by a trustee.

However, Sargent and Howard, with help from others, were able to take over the business in November 1899 trading as S Ockenden & Son with premises in High Street and River Road.

In 1900 Howard took control of the company and was known as a gentleman businessman, like his father. He eventually served as chairman of Arun Urban District Council in 1952.

In 1919, the company took over a builders' merchants they had helped develop before the war. The interwar years did not seem to affect their trade but the River Road forges were affected by changing technology and the decline in sailing ships making the forges redundant. The premises were then used as a badly needed storage unit and in 1936 they purchased Roness Wharf which was soon renamed Arun Wharf. These premises included some of the American aircraft hangers moved from Rustington after WW1 and were used as garages and workshops for the company's fleet of vehicles.

Builders

Given that the population of the town had risen from about 584 in 1801 to 5,950 in 1901, it can be imagined that there was a need for a lot of house-building over the century. Two local house-builders stand out in this development: Snewins and Robert Bushby. Bushby was notorious for referring the Littlehampton Local Board of Health to the appropriate ministry over its failure to maintain and expand the drainage originally installed by the Duke of Norfolk.

The Local Board was incensed and, in the first instance, refused to meet the government inspector sent down to look into the complaint. They then tried to limit his report to covering the particular streets indicated by Bushby and not addressing the town as a whole. In the end the inspector upheld Bushby's complaints and required the Local Board to completely revise its arrangements. In fact, it took about 20 years for this all to be put in place and the town to be supplied with both sewers (draining into the sea at the river mouth!) and piped fresh water.

Bushby was the builder of the Congregational Church in the High Street in 1861. He also installed new foundations in Chichester

Cathedral when a new tower was built. In the first half of the twentieth century Linfield &Sons was a major local builder.

Constable's Brewery

In the second half of the nineteenth century the High Street was dominated by Constable's Brewery. The business directories show that there usually were small breweries operating in different parts of Littlehampton, probably back-room operations serving a one room pub. However, Constables built a large brewery serving a wider area and situated right in the High Street.

The history of the brewery is analysed in Barrett & Greenwood (2020). They say that George Constable owned the Anchor Brewery from 1841 and also the Swallow Brewery in Arundel. He traded as G S Constable and Sons Ltd. The business passed to his son Thomas Constable who expanded the brewery in 1871 to include a tower which dominated the north side of the High Street and was bounded on the east side by Duke Street. Thomas Constable in turn died in October 1885 and left the business to the next generation.

His nephew Archie Constable moved into a house next to the brewery and proceeded both to run the brewery and play an active part in Littlehampton's civic life. He served on the LUDC for many years, including two stints as chairman. He became a county councillor and chairman of the Harbour Commissioners. He was captain of the volunteer fire service, a keen golfer and office-holder in the golf club, as well as a member of the

Illustration 54. A. J. Constable
(Littlehampton Museum Collection)

cricket club. The fountain in the park on the corner of Beach Road and Church Approach was given by him.

The company merged with Henty, another brewer, and closed the Anchor Brewery in Littlehampton in 1917. They traded thereafter as Henty and Constable.

Professional activity

The trade directories show that from the beginning of the nineteenth century Littlehampton had several resident doctors, with one of them, Dr Candy, playing a part in the town's civic life and serving as the first chairman of the Local Board. Over time the town also included a number of lawyers, some of whom appeared regularly for clients in the county court at Arundel. As the data extracted from Kelly's directory in the hospitality section above shows, the number of businesses operating in Littlehampton rose from 103 in 1851 to 677 in 1911.

Of course some Littlehampton people sought employment elsewhere. Famously Benjamin Gray, born in Littlehampton in 1810 and trained as a carpenter, emigrated with his young family to Australia in 1838. His story and the creation of Littlehampton South Australia is to be found in Gammon (1914).

Chapter 7

Schools

There are two strands to the history of schools in Littlehampton, one is about local needs, the other is arguably a form of tourism where wealthy individuals and people in colonial service overseas sent their children to boarding schools by the sea, not least because they wanted the healthiest environment for their children. Private schools were to be found all along the Channel coast. The 1832 Pigot's Directory for Littlehampton shows the town was no exception.

Small schools could easily be opened in someone's dining room and teach reading and writing to local children for a small daily sum. Boarding schools were more difficult, requiring greater capital, but both were relatively commonplace, even in a small town such as Littlehampton was in 1832 (1625 inhabitants).

PROFESSIONAL PERSONS.

'Candy J. H. surgeon
Cox Thos. Philips, boys' day school
Evans Owen, surgeon
Harwood and Overington, ladies' boarding academy
Simpson George, boys' day school
Tidey Miss Ann, professor of music
Tidey J. F. gentlemen's boarding and day academy
Wallington Thomas, surgeon

Illustration 55. Extract from Pigot's Directory

They tended also to be fairly ephemeral, with few lasting as much as ten years. Of course, Rosemead Girls' School was an exception, operating in the town from 1919 to 1995 and continuing elsewhere after that.

Educating local children

At the beginning of the nineteenth century schooling was not compulsory, although it would be by the end of the century. For working class children school was a key economic determinant of their lives. The ability to read, write and do arithmetic was a passport to better jobs and a better life; to be illiterate was to be forced into manual labour with no prospect of any advancement.

Fortunately, wealthier people were well aware of the problem, and occasional donations and bequests ensured that some education was available. The religious bodies also contributed, not least by running Sunday Schools whose aim was a basic education, not centred on religion at that time.

There was no governmental system for schooling before the Education Act of 1870 therefore only a small section of the child population received any form of schooling. Opportunities for a formal education were restricted mainly to town grammar schools, charity schools and dame schools. Boys from well-off families went to grammar schools, girls also went to school but learned instead more domestic accomplishments such as embroidery.

Grammar Schools were mainly civic foundations going back to Tudor times or earlier and in most cases were endowed by rich merchants. The schools were furnished with an income or grant of money, land or other assets which would provide for their continuing support. An example of such a school is Haberdashers' Adam's Grammar School in Shropshire, set up in 1656 by an endowment from William Adams, and supported by the Haberdashers. Newer foundations copied the older grammar schools, took fees and were run on commercial lines advertising their services in newspapers. However, these were often built on precarious finances and failed to survive for very long.

Charity Schools were less formal institutions and were geared towards the poorer sections of society. A key promoter of these was the Society for the Propagation of Christian Knowledge (SPCK) founded in 1699. Their main aim is to spread Christian knowledge. During the 18th century the Society promoted schools for the poor in the 7-11 age group and it is from these schools that the modern concept of primary and secondary education has grown. (UK Parliament website).

The National Society for Promoting Religious Education was founded in 1811.It was primarily set up to improve the education of the poor and sometimes grew up out of the early Sunday schools. Its schools were typically set up by the local vicar and parish council and were widely known as 'National' schools, a term that still survives. The Society aimed to create a national network of schools based on the Church of England.

Private schools of varying kinds existed as well. These were often referred to as 'Dame' schools and were usually run by older ladies or retired soldiers who for a small fee taught the basic 3Rs (reading, writing and arithmetic) to children of the poorer families. As we shall see in the case of Littlehampton, many of these schools lasted only for a short while, due to the retirement or the demise of the teacher.

Early education in Littlehampton

In 1764 Jane Downer of Storrington left a sum of 25s to endow a schoolmaster in Littlehampton. The first master was in post by 1769and by 1833 there were 16 boys and girls in the school. John Corney, who had owned a shipyard on Fisherman's Quay, left an annuity of £18 in his will in 1805 to augment the funding. This was primarily for the teaching of poor boys. This is referred to by an inscription still visible today in the parish church of St Mary's. This says he left:

£18/0/0, which deducting legacy duty is £16/11/12 yearly to a schoolmaster for instructing the poor children of Little Hampton in reading, writing etc to be paid by equal half yearly payments.

A building in Church Street (now the Friends Meeting House) was built by a Mrs Welch who purchased the site in 1835. It became known as a 'Penny a week' school, the pupils paying that amount to cover the running expenses of the place. This building in Church Street was somewhat larger than many of the small front-parlour schools to be found elsewhere in the town. The curriculum would have covered the 3Rs and probably needlework for the girls along with religious instruction.

By 1870 it was connected with the Congregational church and was large enough to split into two separate schools, one for girls and infants and the other for boys, teaching commercial subjects and charging high fees. They became public elementary schools between 1872 and 1874 when there were 110 pupils in all. After the formation of a school board in 1875 the two schools were merged with the National schools.

A schoolmaster who taught there for many years was Henry Lock. He was a remarkable man who, in spite of a modest education, managed to rise some way above his humble beginnings. His father drowned at sea when he was only twelve years old. The family lived in a cottage which was on Island Terrace near the town pond (the site has been redeveloped since) at the end of Church Street. Henry married a schoolteacher and, after leaving the footwear business which had been his previous occupation, he is recorded as being a schoolteacher in 1837.

The Church Street School was closed in 1875 but Lock continued to live in his cottage nearby until his death in 1895. In 1882 he gave a lecture about life in Littlehampton since the end of the Napoleonic Wars (1815). The substance of this was also written down and was re-published by Jack Thompson in his 1983 vol 5 of *The Littlehampton Story*.

National School

In 1846 St Mary's Parish extended its educational activities to establish a National School, for which premises were built on the east side of the church. It was funded by donations, fees and bequests. Charles Rumball was an active vicar who was incumbent at St. Mary's from 1864 to 1895. He invited Thomas Slatford to become Head Teacher of the National School from 1871 to 1875. There was such a close relationship between church and school that the school day began at 9 am with scripture taken by Slatford and ended at 4.15 pm with a service taken by Rumball.

The 1870 Education Act introduced a school system partly funded by government and run by a local Schools Board which had the power to raise a local rate. The schools run under this system were known as 'board' schools. The Littlehampton National School had expanded to develop separate girls' and infants' schools but was struggling financially and in 1875 they were passed over to a newly-created Littlehampton Schools Board. The schools run by the Congregational Church were also merged into the Schools Board and its schools at this time.

The girls' national school moved to the High Street and a new school was built in East Street (this still stands and is used as the Flintstone Centre). The boys were moved to a new building in Connaught Road. This was for many years known just as the

Illustration 56. East Street School 1885
(Greaves Collection)

Connaught Road School, but ultimately became the River Beach School. The junior and infant schools were reunited in 1940 in Elm Grove (since demolished). A senior girls' school was established here at this date and a senior boys' school was created by expanding the buildings on the Connaught Road site.

Roman Catholic School

A Roman Catholic elementary school was founded in 1863, and was conducted in a hired room. A new building was provided by the Duke of Norfolk in 1869 in Irvine Road. In 1872 the school was managed by the mission clergy and the average attendance was 23. This was run by voluntary contributions and fees but by 1878 there was an annual government grant as average attendance rose to over 100 in the 1890s (Victoria County History).

Later the Convent of the Holy Family, was founded in 1914, housed at Aucklands which was situated at the corner of Norfolk Road and Berry Lane. It was a boarding and day school for girls. In 1958 there were 215 girls including 80 boarders. The day girls came from as far as Bognor Regis and Worthing. (*West Sussex Gazette* 18th February 1988) A postcard shows the girls playing tennis on the fields adjacent to the school and another one depicts the dormitories with panels at the side of each bed for privacy and curtains at the foot of the beds. The school closed in 1988 and the building was pulled down. The site is now occupied by housing and all traces of the school have vanished.

Wick and Lyminster

In 1845 an endowed school was opened for 49 children from Lyminster and Rustington, and the schoolmaster was a Mr George Davis. It was built on a site described in the 1838 Tithe Apportionment as a school croft. The site covered a grassy area of nearly half an acre and was owned by Hugh Penfold. Wick Hall now stands on this site and part of it is still used for educational purposes as a nursery.

On the northern edge of Littlehampton on a site situated between the junction of Wick Street and the Worthing Road a school was built in 1878 following the Education Act of 1870. The four acres of land where the school stands was owned by Eton College and has been since the time of Henry VI. The school at the time had places for 36 children and the cost of the build was £2,500. The head was William Strong who was only 26 years' old. (Daggett 1995)

Illustration 57. Lyminster School 1909
(Greaves Collection)

Private Schools

In Littlehampton in the nineteenth century there were no large institutions such as there were in the bigger cities, instead there were numerous smaller educational establishments, some of which lasted longer than others. One of the main reasons that Littlehampton was considered a popular destination for children was of course, the sea air and possessing: 'a mild and salubrious air, 59 miles from London by road and 62 by the London Brighton and South Coast railway' (Kelly's Directory 1890). Generally, there was a heavy presence of such schools all along the Channel coast.

Many parents whose work was connected to the colonies were happy to be able to send their children down to the south coast and settle them in schools where they could also board. Female boarding schools were classified as being solely for 'ladies'. Boarding school fees were expensive, so only the well-off middle classes could afford to send their offspring away.

Throughout the nineteenth century there was a plethora of small schools of all kinds, not necessarily boarding schools, as the extract from the 1832 Pigot's Directory shows. Amongst the women of Littlehampton who were running schools there is listed: Miss Jemima Gales had a Ladies School in 1851. Miss Eliza Cobden ran a boarding school in 1855. Mrs Georgina Whitmarsh ran a Ladies Boarding School thought to be located in South Terrace in 1855.

Among the longer-lived and better-established schools was that of John Grix, who is commemorated on a plaque in St Mary's church. He was principal of Surrey House School for 20 years, from 1841-1861. It was an imposing building which would have had wonderful views of the sea. The school was in existence from 1839 to 1890.

The school was prominent in Littlehampton for many years. It was considered a popular establishment and many of the sons of leading residents in West Sussex were boarders. There were also weekly boarders and many of these became leading and well-known townsmen of Littlehampton. There were no organised games or sports at the school. Football was played with few rules and later cricket was played in a more conventional manner.

Mr Grix had two daughters and the elder one married the assistant master, Mr George Neame. When John Grix died, Neame took over the running of the school and maintained its prestigious status for many years.

At the time of John Grix's death an article appeared in the *Brighton Gazette* on Thursday August 8th, 1861. The article was headed 'The Uncertainty of Life' and went on to say 'At the Parish Church on Sunday Mr John Grix who, in company with his two daughters, after taking Communion, was seized with a fit of apoplexy on returning to his pew and led to his death a few hours' later'. It would seem that John Grix was popular and held in high esteem as the plaque in the church was erected by his late pupils 'as a tribute of their respect and affection'.

Mr Neame had a large family but none of his children took up the succession. When Neame became too old to carry on the school the house reverted to being private and was occupied by Lady Percy St Maur (Robinson and Heward 1933).

Illustration 58. Miss Boniface taught at East Street Girls' School for more than 50 years, more than half serving as headmistress (Greaves Collection)

According to the *Brighton Gazette* of 1848 a Miss Burton brought her 'celebrated and long-established school for young ladies has been removed from Boulogne to the largest house in this place for an indefinite period, waiting a settled state of things in France'. An auction notice of 1856 suggests that she occupied 18 – 20 South Terrace. Although the houses appear to be separate, they were built so that they could be used as a single unit and over the years have been used at various times as a boarding school, a hotel and a nursing home.

Miss Burton was eventually succeeded there by the Rev Philpott, who ran a boys' school in the premises during the 1870s. Philpott was famous for being a cricket fanatic. He could be relied upon to supply a school team, or a strong school contingent to form a scratch Littlehampton team, at the drop of a hat. The newspapers were full of match reports at the time. Philpott was also a contributor to communal life and served on the Local Board and on the Board of the East Preston Union. The Bishop of Chichester offered him the living of South Bersted in1875 which he accepted and closed down his school. He died in 1889.

Edmund Peacock Toy came to settle in Littlehampton from Wiltshire and founded a boy's school. His family were involved in his enterprise including his wife Emily who was a trained teacher and came from Brighton. Two of his four children, Emily and Ethel, also devoted themselves to education.

Old school reports preserved by relatives of past scholars show that botany, other sciences, mathematics, English and all aspects of business studies were taught. Esperanto was also taught, and used when one of the older boys was able to communicate with shipwrecked sailors. The two daughters, Emily and Maud, set up a school at Rosamond House, later it moved to Brockenhurst House School in Arundel Road. A building there still keeps the same name.

Edmund Toy's school is commemorated by a plaque in the Lecture Hall of the Congregational church (now the United Church) in the High Street. This plaque reads: 'This tablet was erected by the old scholars in affectionate remembrance of Edmund P Toy who for upwards of 50 years 1868-1918 was the principal of the Littlehampton Middle Class School held in this building'. Although Toy's school was a private venture, classes were held on the various premises of the Congregational Church in the High Street.

Edenmore Prep School came to Littlehampton from Surbiton. It was a boarding and day school for boys and claimed to give a thorough training in all subjects. Boys prepared for entrance examinations to public schools and for other examinations required by parents. The school claimed its fees were moderate. Its headmaster was Jocelyn Hill. The school stood in its own grounds in Granville Road and for many years was the premises occupied by St. Hilda's School, mentioned previously.

Dorset House School in East Street moved to Littlehampton from Elstree, Herts, in 1886 and was almost exclusively a cramming school for the Navy until 1905 when it became a general preparatory school. In 1910 the Littlehampton Town Guide described it as a preparatory school for boys. The guide notes that Edmund A Hollingberry (Rugby School and St John's Oxford) was amongst the highly qualified scholars to provide education for boys between the age of seven and fourteen.

The school stood in five acres and contained a cricket and football pitch, tennis courts and a gymnasium. Instruction included scripture, classics, English, French, geography, history and mathematics. In 1963 the school moved to premises in Bury, including an old mansion set in beautiful grounds.

Another of the more permanent private schools was Groombridge House School situated in Norfolk Road. This opened as Pelham House School in 1907 by Mrs Braithwaite, before changing to Groombridge House under John Langfield, who ran the school with his two sisters. The building still stands and from postcards we can see it had a rather sumptuous dining room.

The school was known for its singing and frequently entered choirs in local choral competitions. It was also active in the community, raising money for charities, especially in WWI. Its exam successes were reported in the Littlehampton Gazette, including at least one scholarship to Oxford. John Langfield died in April 1935, but his sisters continued to run the school with a new headmaster. However, as far as we can tell the school was moved to 18 – 20 South Terrace (which had immediately previously been Hillyers

Hotel) in 1938. We have not been able to find any trace of them later than that. Groombridge House was taken over as the Air Raid Precautions (ARP) centre and was busy dishing out gas masks in 1938.

The school was also connected, through one of its domestic staff, with a curious case of poison pen letters. The details are recounted in Littlehampton Libels (Hilliard 2017)

Illustration 59. Part of Rosemead School
(Littlehampton Museum Collection)

Nearby, was one of the larger and better known private educational establishments in Littlehampton: Rosemead School. A school called Winterton was set up in Winterton Lodge in Littlehampton in 1913 by Mrs Hiscock and Miss Stowell (Winterton Lodge still exists as apartments. It is on the corner of Goda Road and East Street). In 1915 Winterton School moved to the house called Rosemead in what was originally the Hollingbury Boys' School. This house was just a short distance from Winterton Lodge.

In June 1919 Miss Ruth Young and Miss Nita Sharpe who met whilst teaching at the French school in Bray, Ireland, decided to run a school together in England. They acquired the Winterton

School but decided to start afresh and called the school Rosemead after the house in which it was to exist. The school opened in June 1919 and began with 8 boarders and 17 day pupils. The fees were to be 30 to 33 guineas per term. Amongst the usual classes sea bathing and horse riding were offered.

By 1922 there were over 100 pupils and the school had expanded to other sites in Littlehampton including a house named Roxwell on the corner of Norfolk Road and also Conway in Beach Road. These were to house the boarders. Buildings were added on the Rosemead site in 1923. The girls could often be seen walking around that part of Littlehampton in their distinctive checked uniforms. It served an area from Chichester to Worthing and Chiltington in the north. In 1963 it expanded to include the land and buildings of the former Dorset House School. In 1995 the school merged with Lavant School near Chichester and moved to their premises (Victoria County History and Morgan Wilson 2000).

Postscript

There are no longer any boarding or other private schools in Littlehampton, the few survivors having moved away from the coast. The state sector continued to evolve however. In 1958 the senior boys' school moved to Elm Grove Road (then known as Andrew Cairns County Secondary school). The juniors moved to the Connaught Road buildings. The infants remained at Elm Grove Road, moving to adjacent buildings in 1967 (then called Elm Grove Infant School).

The Elm Grove senior girls' school moved into the former junior buildings vacated in1958, and in 1961 became the Maud Allen School. The two secondary schools merged into one in 1972 and became the Littlehampton Community College. This building was pulled down in 2009 and a brand-new building erected now named an Academy.

Chapter 8

Churches

The role of religion and religious organisations in society has changed a great deal over the time of this study. At the beginning of the nineteenth century the Anglican church had a central part in the way society was organised, a part which extended to some degree into the civil administration of the parish. Under the Poor Law, for example, the parish council had oversight of the arrangements for poor relief and the right to levy a rate upon the inhabitants.

The nineteenth century would see a great deal of activity including the expansion of the Anglican churches as the population of Littlehampton expanded. But it would also see the arrival of other major religious organisations, including the Wesleyan Methodists and the Roman Catholic church. A Congregational Church was built in the High Street and played a major role in the town thereafter, and for a time the town also had representation of the Salvation Army and the Plymouth Brethren, as well as the primitive Methodists. Oddly, for a town which belonged to a famously Roman Catholic landowner, the Duke of Norfolk, the town had no Roman Catholic church until 1863.

The rapid development of churches and religious groups in nineteenth century Littlehampton was to be followed by a slow decline in the twentieth, accelerating in the second half of the century, and a disappearance of smaller organisations as well as the disposal of a significant number of churches.

St Mary's Church

St Mary the Virgin is the Anglican parish church of Littlehampton. The site where the present building stands has been a place of worship since Saxon times. According to Jack Thompson the site was possibly chosen because it was the highest part of the town while much of the area in early times was very wet and swampy. The first recorded church of 1110 was taken down in 1824 as the growing population required a bigger place of worship. It was rebuilt in 1826 by architect George Draper, unfortunately little of the old church was retained except for the font and east window.

Illustration 60. St Mary's Church c1820
(Greaves Collection)

About 50 years later during the time of the then vicar Rev Charles Rumball a brick chancel and vestries were added but for reasons unknown the 14th century east window was discarded and the brickwork dumped in the corner of the churchyard. Some years later, in early 1930, the vicar discovered the stones while clearing up and totally unaware of their significance gave them away. Fortunately, the recipient realised what they were and immediately handed them back and the window was later incorporated in the tower of the building.

Rev Rumball held the parish for over 30 years and made many changes. Soon after he came to St Mary's in 1864 he became influenced by Anglo-Catholicism. He introduced high church rituals to the services, something which was not welcomed by some of the congregation. As a consequence, after a heated meeting in March 1875 two groups left St Mary's and went on to build themselves new churches: St Saviour's, a Free Episcopalian Church in New Road, built in 1878 by Snewin Bros (demolished in 1980), and St John's (The Fisherman's Church) built in 1877 by Robert Bushby in Pier Road/Fisherman's Hard (demolished in 1976).

During his incumbency Rev Rumball obtained financing and built a vicarage nearby. He also expanded the chancel of the church and added ancillary buildings. On the 25th anniversary of his appointment, in 1889, his parishioners presented him with a piano and recognition of his work. Aside from being an active parish priest, Rev Rumball was also active in town affairs. He sat for some time on the Local Board of Health and chaired the Schools Board which ran the National

Illustration 61. Rev Charles Rumball (Peter Walton)

schools in Littlehampton. He died in July 1895 at the age of 65. He was buried in St Albans.

His replacement was Rev Bebbington, who, virtually as soon as he was appointed, was the subject of a challenge as to his high church tendencies. Some parishioners felt that the diocese had deliberately sought to maintain high church practices. In 1900 a Mr Madden chose the occasion of the Easter vestry meeting to propose a motion calling on the Bishop of Chichester to prevent 'Romish practices' including the use of a processional cross, vestments and communion wafers[9]. The motion failed with only Mr Madden and his seconder supporting it and the rest of the vestry voting against.

The following year Mr Madden, undeterred, invited the vestry to vote in favour of a motion censuring the Bishop of Chichester for not stopping illegal practices at St Mary's. Rev Bebbington, in the chair, mildly noted that he did not think the vestry had the power to censure its bishop. Mr Madden settled for a motion to propose holding a public meeting, but as in the previous year the vestry was unanimous in its opposition. The vicar may conceivably have wondered why Mr Madden did not seek a rite more congenial to him elsewhere.

In 1934, St Mary's church was again rebuilt by designer Randolf Blacking (from the outside then the middle taken out said Margaret Baker who was at that time living in Winterton Lodge) although some of the ornaments were retained. Fortunately, the 14th century window was able to be restored and was this time placed in the west wall of the tower beneath the clock where it remains to this day. Nikolaus Pevsner in his *Buildings of England* called it "eerie disembodied gothic" (also referred to as 'Pastry-cook Gothic').

St Saviour's Church

This church in New Road was formed by the Free Episcopalian group, the first group of members who had broken away from St. Mary's Church in 1875. It should be noted that the Church of England has for centuries included within its congregation people who prefer a ritualised and ornate approach to services and those who prefer a simple, unadorned style.

Famously the protests by Martin Luther against the Roman Catholic church of his time were of this general nature. In Britain,

[9] These would be regarded as fairly unexceptional today, with objections being more to 'bells and smells' in contemporary high church ritual.

John Wesley is an example of someone breaking away from the established church to set up a simpler ministry.

In the nineteenth century there were other splits within the Church of England. In particular the Free Church was established in the middle of the century in protest at the influence of the Oxford Movement which wanted rites nearer to those of the Roman Catholic church – then as now known as the High Church. Those who preferred simpler rites – known as the Low Church – did not accept these, and some congregations were incensed enough to create a separate Episcopal church, the Free Church. This had bishops and followed Church of England principles but was not part of the established church.

St Saviour's was intended to be part of this Low Church movement. Completed 20th August 1877 by Snewin Bros on leased land, this church did not in fact survive for long. In 1890 it ceased to operate as a church. The premises were then sold and for the next few years became a theatre known variously as the Victoria Hall and then the Jubilee Hall. The premises were also used for sales of furniture and for storage until they were put up for sale again and purchased in 1896 by the Wesleyan Methodists.

St John's Church

This church was formed by the second group of members who had broken away from St Mary's Church in 1875 following a disagreement over the high church rituals being introduced by Rev Rumball. This was known as "The Fisherman's Church" and was built in Pier Road by Robert Bushby in 1877. Being a temporary timber structure, the church was never consecrated; possibly it was hoped it would soon be replaced. However, the church had a loyal congregation and worship continued for many years.

Following the death of Rev Jamieson, the church fell on hard times. For a few years the church continued under the wing of St James the Great, Arundel Road with visiting ministers but was closed after the Second World War. The premises were put up for auction and were bought by Percy Davison an antique dealer who had plans to turn it into a playhouse. However, this did not materialise and eventually the County Council took over and it became a Youth Theatre Workshop. It was demolished in 1976 with the land now a car park to the rear of Lifeboat station.

All Saints Parish Church, Wick

An Anglican mission church was built in 1881 in Wick Street in what was the parish of Lyminster, a part that was hived off to Littlehampton when the parish of Wick was subsumed into Littlehampton UDC in 1901. The architect of the mission church was George Edmund Street, the designer of the Royal Courts of Justice. In 1973 the area was constituted as a separate parish. Originally known just as the mission church, it later changed its name to All Saints.

All Saints is a typical chapelry of the period built of brick and flints with lancet windows. The church used the late nineteenth century practice of putting a transfer on plain glass imitating stained glass. Although of no particular artistic merit, All Saints' windows are a rare survival of such cheap church decorations. There is a bellcote on the east gable. Like many churches where alterations have been carried out, the original chimney has been removed and changes made to the west doorway (Elleray1991). Standing on an elevated position in Wick Street it is reached by several steps and is adjacent to Lyminster school. Today this is an active thriving church with a large congregation (Sussex Parish Churches.org).

St James the Great Church

In 1898/99 as part of the development of the area around East Ham Road, a mission church under the authority of St Mary's Church was erected there, under the initiative of Rev Bebbington. Initially built of corrugated iron, the little church of St James was affectionately nicknamed "Tin Jim". Moves were soon afoot to build a more substantial structure and by 1908 a new church had been built. It remained a subsidiary of St Mary's for the next 21 years. The old mission church building was retained and used as the church hall until after the Second World War when a new hall was built; "Tin Jim" was finally demolished in 1967.

By 1929 the growth of the town warranted two separate parishes and St James became the church of the new parish and the curate was elevated to the status of vicar. St John's, the Fisherman's Church in Pier Road, then came under the wing of this new parish of St James (Thompson 1974, page 96). When Rev Bebbington died in the 1930s, a monument celebrating his ministry was erected in St James's church.

Congregational Church

In 1858 it was felt there was a need for another non-Anglican church in Littlehampton so Littlehampton resident Samuel Evershed, Deacon of the Independent Church in Arundel (where the Independents/Congregationalists met), and Thomas Duke of Wick approached Samuel Morley of London (MP for Bristol) who was at the time staying in Littlehampton, to ask for his help in building a chapel in Littlehampton.

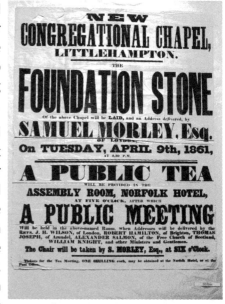

Land on the corner of Arundel Road and High Street, at that time leased by William Latter and consisting of thatched farm buildings, became available and was acquired on a 99-year lease from the Duke of Norfolk. Unfortunately, Samuel Evershed died in November 1859 and the scheme to build a chapel

Illustration 62. Poster for Congregational Church 1861 (Littlehampton Museum Collection)

almost came to an end but in 1860 his son Edward revived the project, eventually becoming the first secretary of the new church. Robert Bushby, one of Littlehampton's more prolific builders of the second half of the nineteenth century, was the builder.

On Tuesday 9th April 1861 the Foundation Stone was laid by Mr Morley together with a glass bottle containing information about the church building, services and names of people involved plus a copy of the *West Sussex Gazette* and the *Patriot* newspaper.

The Church, completed in October 1861, was built in the Early Decorated English style at a cost of £1140 with seating for 275. The *Brighton Gazette* described it as having 'the prettiest exterior and interior of any building in the town'. It was 55ft in length, while the width at the nave 30ft, and at the transept 35ft. At the rear was a school measuring 33ft by 19ft. The entire cost and expenses had been raised by the year of its completion.

The Rev William Knight of Egham Hill, Surrey, was appointed as the first minister of the new Congregational church. He remained at the church for 20 years and the Knight Hall built later was named in his memory.

In 1862 the manse was built adjacent to the church at a cost of £650 using the same architect and builder. Unfortunately, the manse was destroyed at 2.05pm on Sunday 9th August 1942 during a WW2 daylight raid by enemy planes and tragically both Rev and Mrs Hailstone were killed along with two friends who were staying with them. Both the Lecture Hall and the Knight Hall were also badly damaged in the same raid. In 1949 the manse was rebuilt with funds from the War Damage Commission.

The public Lecture Hall was built in 1865 at a cost of £639. Although the premises were part of the church, the hall was also used frequently for concerts and public meetings of all kinds, playing a significant role in Littlehampton communal activities. Henry Lock may have given talks there. In 1865 Edmund P Toy set up his Littlehampton Middle Class School in the building which ran for 50 years (there is a commemorative plaque in hall). In 1893 plans were drawn up for alterations and improvements which included replacing the lancet window on the west wall facing the High Street with the present rose window.

In 1924 Miss Kathleen Cocksedge started the 1st Littlehampton Brownies and Guide Company in the church. She was the first Brown Owl and continued for 43 years until her death in 1967.

Much later, in the 1970s, the decline in church attendance resulted in two amalgamations, under the latter of which in 1980 what had started out as the Congregational Church became Littlehampton United Church, bringing together the congregations of all the Free churches.

St Catherine's Catholic Church

Illustration 63. St Catherine's Church with St Mary's in the background
(Greaves Collection)

St Catherine of Alexandria Roman Catholic Church is sited towards the southern end of Beach Road. Designed by M E Hadfield the church was built at a cost of £4000 in 1863 on land given to the church by the Duke of Norfolk (Elleray 1991). Most of the cost was borne by Minna, Dowager Duchess of Norfolk who had the church built in memory of her late husband Henry 14th Duke of Norfolk. The Duke died in 1860 at the age of 45, having inherited the title only four years previously. Enlargements were made to the church in 1884 and 1904. Part of the diocese of Arundel and Brighton, the building is now Grade II listed (Sussex Parish Churches.org).

Wesleyan Methodist Chapel

Methodism manifested in Littlehampton in the early nineteenth century (1816) with services being held outdoors in the town centre, in front of the Manor House. Using a drum head for a reading desk, worship was led by a sergeant and men from the barracks in Western Road. Later a room was opened for services by a boat builder named Stow. They then moved to Judith Hutchings' house in a court off Church Street. In 1820 a large upper room was taken holding about 50 people at 1 Montague Row in River Road.

Through the efforts of a local preacher named Hore, the Wesleyan chapel in Terminus Road was built in 1825. The chapel was enlarged twice, the second time being in 1866 when it was renovated and new seating provided; later the side galleries were removed and the old pulpit replaced with a rostrum.

Pew rents were a regular source of income from 1825 to 1937. Although the premises were registered as a place of worship from February 1854 it was not until later that the premises were authorised to conduct marriages.

Over time, given the rapid growth of Littlehampton, it was deemed necessary to find bigger premises in a more central location so St Saviours Church in New Road was purchased on 26th January 1896 for £830. £500 was spent on improvements which included partitioning off the rear to provide a school room. The first service was held on 5th August 1896 and it remained a place of worship until 1980.

The old Wesleyan chapel in Terminus Road was sold for £460. The building was later used as auction rooms until a forecourt was added and it became the Clifton Café, at one time owned by Anita Roddick's family.

In 1898 when all debts from the purchase of the former St. Saviours had been cleared, the Trustees purchased the hall (built 1887) adjoining the church. Initially this was let as a furniture depository for an annual rent of £35. However, following alterations and renovation the hall was first used by the church in 1915 and renamed Wesley Hall. In 1926 the Trustees purchased the freehold of the land for £250 from the Duchy of Norfolk Estate.

On 1st July 1980 the Littlehampton United Reformed Church and Littlehampton Methodist Church officially became The Littlehampton United Church. As the High Street premises were deemed the more suitable, all the artefacts and adornments including the pews etc from New Road were moved to the High Street premises.

Primitive Methodist Mission

The Primitive Methodists were an early nineteenth century secession from the Wesleyan Methodists who were particularly successful in evangelising agricultural and industrial outdoor meetings. In 1875 a Littlehampton Mission was formed and by the following year 1876 Wick Chapel in Wick Street was opened (Sussex Parish Churches.org).

The Littlehampton Methodism handbook 1800 – 1980 collated by Ron Sylvester and edited by Rev David Clark states that a circuit reorganisation took place and Wick and Rustington came into the Littlehampton/Worthing Mission with 34 members. This had increased to 194 members by 1884.

By 1890 all debts on the premises had been paid and at the Quarterly Meeting a request was made to pay the Super-intendent's "trainage" from Worthing to Littlehampton as he was unable to walk that distance. At the February Chapel Anniversary meeting in Worthing the Superintendent was reported to say:

"There was a great need for the Gospel at Wick, for many people there were as ignorant and wicked as the people in Africa." (See also Daggett 1995)

In 1900 at a Quarterly Meeting a proposal was made to unite with the Bible Christians; this was agreed unanimously. The membership in 1904 was 18 and by 1925 down to 11. The Primitive Methodists, United Methodists and Wesleyan Methodists joined together in 1932 to become The Methodist Church and in 1937 Wick and Rustington came under the Chichester/Bognor circuit.

Although the Primitive Methodist story had ended, the Society at Wick continued with Sunday school and many activities i.e. Youth Groups and Woman's Own. However, this was not to last as in 1968 West Sussex County Council required the premises for a road widening scheme so the building was demolished.

Littlehampton Baptist Church

The church was formed in 1907 by the Rev Charles Ingram in the home of Mrs Hilda Harvey, of the shipbuilding family. The church joined the Kent and Sussex Baptist Association in 1908 and, at the request of the Mission, their secretary Rev F J Flatt became pastor at the church in January 1909.

There was no hall in which to hold services but eventually it was possible to hire the Terminus Hall which was used as a cinema during the week. However, they obtained a lease of their present site in Fitzalan Road from the Duchy of Norfolk, and a congregation member, R Bowes, drew up plans for the church. The foundation stone was laid in 1910 and church services in the new building started later that year.

Rev Flatt left in 1921, following which there was a three-year inter-regnum without a permanent pastor. The parish decided that recruitment would be helped by the provision of accommodation and a house was acquired in 1924, as well as a new pastor. The parish went on to build a school hall in 1939.

Cemetery

The parish cemetery was next to St Mary's church, but as the town expanded, and other churches were established, the town needed more space. The Duke of Norfolk offered what was known as Corney's Field in 1871 as a multi-denominational cemetery. Rev Rumball was reported as not being enthusiastic, given the distance from St Mary's, but the offer was accepted and the new cemetery opened in 1872 with two chapels.

The cemetery is on Horsham Road (the extension of East Street) and was really on the outskirts of Littlehampton to the north-east. Later the A259 through road was built just north of it. It has been extended several times since 1872.

In this cemetery can be found the grave of Catherine Parnell, who died in Littlehampton. Mrs Parnell initially became notorious as Kittie O'Shea, the mistress of Charles Parnell the prominent Irish politician. She subsequently obtained a divorce and married Parnell, but the scandal of the affair ended his political career.

Illustration 64. Kittie O'Shea's gravestone
(DavidTwinn)

Chapter 9

Conclusion

This book has attempted to cover the story of Littlehampton from 1800 to 1940: from a fishing village of 584 souls to a peak of 11,412 in 1921 as a modern seaside resort. It started out the journey as the fiefdom of the Duchy of Norfolk, it became a busy harbour and ship-building centre in the nineteenth century and then a seaside destination. Along the way, in time with the evolution of central and local government in the UK, it ceased to be governed by the Duchy who eventually sold it.

It can be seen as slowly slipping the influence of Arundel, both physically in terms of the harbour and legally as independent local government was built up from the middle of the nineteenth century. Not that the influence of the Duchy was not beneficial to Littlehampton and the dukes complicit in building up the town.

The first boost to the town was the Napoleonic wars which caused numbers of troops to be based there. They also influenced the construction of the Chichester Canal and the Wey and Arun Canal as a means of transporting goods between Portsmouth and London. The growth of the UK economy in the wake of the industrial revolution meant there was a burgeoning coastal trade which interconnected, using Littlehampton, with Sussex, Surrey and London.

The port's prosperity grew and was boosted further by the railway, which arrived in 1846. From 1863 there was extensive trade with France and the Channel Islands. But while steam power had brought the railway, it eventually took away the shipping and the port declined towards the end of the nineteenth century.

The Duchy was in effect the mainspring of Littlehampton's evolution to be a resort. The fact that both the 13th and 14th Dukes kept a household in Littlehampton for significant periods of their lives was probably a major factor in their approach. Beach Town became a centre for the health benefits of the sea. These spread to a wider audience when the railway revolutionised travel, making it incomparably faster and cheaper.

In the second half of the century the resort became accessible to many more and so other people arrived to cater for the needs of the visitor. This unplanned evolution was much helped by the 15th Duke of Norfolk who presided over the second half of the nineteenth century and gave generously to help the town develop its infrastructure. Different denominations of church became established as did the educational infrastructure.

The creation of the Littlehampton Urban District Council in 1894 signalled a more cohesive attempt to organise and improve the town. The First World War created a hiatus but did not disturb the town as much as might have been imagined, with resort activity continuing unabated. After the war the Council made more attempts to improve the entertainment infrastructure, but was caught between the competing pressures of developing sewerage and water schemes to cope with its expanding boundaries and building entertainment facilities.

The period was rich in symbols of the change in power and influence. For example, in 1800 the Harbour Commissioners were based in Arundel, in 1938 a new railway bridge cut Arundel off definitively as a port. In 1800 Littlehampton was owned entirely by the Duchy of Norfolk, in 1939 the Duchy sold its last holdings in the town. The Manor House was built by the 12th Duke in 1827 but owned and occupied by Littlehampton Council from 1933.

References

Barrett, L. & Greenwood, H. (2020) *The George Inn Littlehampton – the true story*

Brown, C. (1991) *The Children's Paradise*, Littlehampton Museum

Daggett, W (1995) *Wick before 1900,* Littlehampton Local History Society, Littlehampton

Elleray, D Robert (1991) *Littlehampton – a Pictorial History*, Phillimore, Chichester

Elleray, D Robert (2006) *Sussex Theatres – an illustrated Survey and Gazetteer* c1750-2000, Optimus Books, Worthing

Eyles, A, Gray, F & Readman, A (1996) *Cinema West Sussex – the first hundred years*, Phillimore, Chichester

Farrant, J (1972) *The Railway and the Cross-Channel Steamers*, Littlehampton UDC

Gammon, Alan (2014) *The Benjamin Gray Story*, Gammon, Littlehampton

Goodwin, John (1985) *The Military Defence of West Sussex*, Middleton Press, Midhurst Sussex

Gray, Nicholas (2021) *Hillyard, the man, his boats and their sailors*, Lodestar Books, London

Hilliard, Christopher (2017) *The Littlehampton Libels – a miscarriage of justice and mystery about words in 1920s England*, Oxford University Press, Oxford

Lansdell, Gwen (2010) 'Time for a Quick One' in *Time for a Quick One and Other Matters*, Littlehampton Local History Society (LLHS), Littlehampton

Phillips, Peregrine (1778) *A sentimental diary, kept in an excursion to Little Hampton, near Arundel, and to Brighthelmstone, in Sussex*, reproduction ECCO

Robinson, E. &Heward, J.S. (1933) *Reminiscences of Littlehampton*, Natural Science and Archaeological Society, Littlehampton

Thompson, H.J.F. (1974) *Little Hampton Long Ago*, Thompson, Littlehampton

Thompson, H.J.F. (1983) *The Littlehampton Story: the early nineteenth century* (No 5), Littlehampton Printers

Victoria County History: *Littlehampton and District* (2009), C.P.Lewis (ed) *A History of the County of Sussex* Vol 2 Part 2, Institute of Historical research/Boydell & Brewer, Woodbridge

Wilson, Morgan P (2000) *Rosemead: Memories of a School*, Gresham Books, Isle of Wight

Wiseman, I (2016) *A Narrative of Littlehampton Golf Club*, Mimeo

Littlehampton 1800 to 1940

Index